VEGETARIAN COOKING MADE EASY

This book is intended particularly for those who wish to prepare vegetarian dishes quickly and yet still obtain full nutriment and enjoyment. All the recipes have been used in the well-known guest house run by the author's parents at Frinton-on-Sea.

The value of a food reform diet as outlined in these recipes cannot be overrated. The high consumption of hard fats, such as butter, rich cream, lard, meat fats and other animal fats, is undoubtedly among the causes of the high incidence of deaths from coronary thrombosis and hardening of the arteries. It is an undisputed fact that these fats can produce a dangerous level of cholesterol (thickening of the blood) in the blood stream.

A well-balanced diet can easily be devised from the recipes in this book. Coupled with a constructive outlook on life generally, they will help to promote good health all the year round.

VEGETARIAN COOKING MADE EASY

by

VERONICA VEZZA

Foreword by
RONALD LIGHTOWLER

Secretary of the London Vegetarian Society

Published by
Melvin Powers
WILSHIRE BOOK COMPANY
12015 Sherman Road
No. Hollywood, California 91605
Telephone: (213) 875-1711 / 983-1105

First published 1970
Copyright © Veronica Vezza

Printed by

HAL LEIGHTON PRINTING COMPANY
P.O. Box 3952
North Hollywood, California 91605
Telephone: (213) 983-1105

Printed in the United States of America
ISBN 0-87980-171-9

FOREWORD

It gives me great pleasure to write a brief foreword to Veronica's book of vegetarian recipes. During the last few years there has been quite a spate of vegetarian recipe books, and each of these has made an unique contribution calculated to help in destroying the false notion that meals without flesh, fish or fowl are necessarily monotonous and lacking in variety.

The author is the daughter of Lillian and Aldo Vezza, whose vegetarian guest house, Sandy Point, at Frinton-on-Sea, Essex, has rightly come to be regarded as one of the best of its kind. Two factors, judging from appreciative comments one has heard repeatedly through the years, have commended Sandy Point to its many guests; these are the welcome friendly atmosphere of the place and its generous and attractive catering.

Now the general public are being given the opportunity of enjoying favourite recipes devised in the Sandy Point kitchen, and from personal experience I can assure them that they will not be disappointed. The simple presentation of the recipes should make this a very popular book with busy people.

RONALD LIGHTOWLER
Secretary of the London Vegetarian Society

CONTENTS

INTRODUCTION

Many vegetarian recipe books have been written and published, each one admirably presented. The meals suggested are in every way tasteful and nutritious, but for the busy housewife or business girl there are other dishes which can be prepared simply, in the minimum time, and which yet provide full nutriment and enjoyment. In order to make these dishes more widely known, and encouraged by the appreciation of many Sandy Point guests of the recipes of the meals provided there, our daughter Veronica decided to write this book of our favourite recipes.

The value of a food reform diet as outlined in these recipes cannot be overrated. The high consumption of hard fats, such as butter, rich cream, lard, meat fats and other animal fats, is undoubtedly among the causes of the high incidence of deaths from coronary thrombosis and hardening of the arteries. It is an undisputed fact that these fats can produce a dangerous level of cholesterol (thickening of the blood) in the blood stream.

It will be noted that all the fats recommended for use in these recipes are from the vegetable family, i.e., corn oil, sunflower oil, etc. The use of these vegetable oils actually brings about a decrease of cholesterol in the blood, and the risk of overweight is also considerably reduced.

A well-balanced diet can easily be devised from all the recipes in this book. Coupled with a constructive outlook on life generally, they will help to keep you fit and active. Besides enjoying nutritious and tasty food, you will be assured of very good health all the year round.

An example which can well be followed to much advantage is to take a glass of unsweetened fruit juice on rising. For breakfast, soaked dried fruit with wheatgerm, sprinkled with groundnuts, or a dish of the wonderful Muesli; wholewheat toast, using very little butter or well covered with corn oil margarine; China tea.

At midday a luncheon with a goodly amount of conservatively cooked green and root vegetables. (Conservative cooking simply means cooking the vegetables in a minimum amount of unsalted water, bringing to the boil quickly and simmering for about twenty minutes.) Potatoes can be cooked in their jackets, by roasting in a little corn oil, or by baking or creaming. (For creaming, of course, the potatoes are peeled after cooking.) Cooking this way retains all the essential valuable salts, and in potatoes particularly the starch content is reduced very considerably. For protein, choose one of the many savouries and a little sauce. End with a dessert as recommended.

For the evening meal: soup if desired, a large mixed salad always, with 100 per cent stone-ground wholewheat bread; end with one of the many wholewheat cakes. Of course, if more convenient the cooked meal can be switched to the evening.

At Sandy Point, we follow a simple set of rules. These are: use only first-grade wholesome ingredients (which, whenever possible, are compost-grown flours, fruits and vegetables) free from artificial colourings and preservatives. Where necessary to use alternatives, use dried or frozen foods in preference to canned, with the exception of the canned foods of such well-known manufacturers as Hunzana Ltd., Mapletons, Granose, Eustace Miles and others. Bread and cakes and pastries of course are made of 100 per cent or 81 per cent wholewheat flours or a mixture of both. Potatoes, whether baked, roasted or creamed, should always be cooked in their skins. Custards should be made from fresh free-range eggs. Nuts should be freshly ground. Make full use of Agar Agar for all jellifying. These are just a few basic essential hints. Commonsense will guide you in others. Prepare your meals with enthusiasm and love, with the wonderful knowledge that not a single living creature had to be sacrificed for the preparation of these meals, and you will be rewarded with praise and delight from your friends and families.

Good cooking.

LILLIAN AND ALDO VEZZA

SOUPS AND SAUCES

TOMATO SOUP

Ingredients:

2 onions	1 lb tomatoes
2 pints vegetable stock	corn oil
2 tablespoons tomato purée	1 oz flour
milk	

Method:

Peel and chop the onions and cook in corn oil until just tender. Skin the tomatoes and chop, add to the onions and cook for five more minutes. Put in a saucepan with the stock and tomato purée blended with the flour and cook for 35 minutes. Sieve or liquidize, return to the pan, add the milk and seasoning and heat gently.

CREAM OF MUSHROOM SOUP

Ingredients:

½ lb mushrooms	2 onions
1 pint stock	1 oz flour
1 egg yolk	seasoning
½ pint milk	2 oz margarine

Method:

Wash and cut the mushrooms, peel and chop the onions and cook both in stock until tender. Melt the margarine and stir in the flour, add the milk and cook for few minutes, add to the soup and liquidize or sieve. Return to the saucepan and stir in the egg yolk and heat gently.

LEEK SOUP

Ingredients:

8 small leeks
corn oil
top of milk
seasoning

2 potatoes
2 pints onion stock
chopped parsley

Method:

Wash the leeks and cut into pieces; cook in corn oil for five minutes. Add the stock and chopped potatoes and cook until tender. Rub through a sieve and liquidize. Return to the saucepan and heat, adding the top of milk and seasoning. Serve with chopped parsley.

ONION SOUP

Ingredients:

¾ lb onions
1 oz flour
seasoning

corn oil
2 pints onion stock
top of milk

Method:

Peel and chop the onions and cook in corn oil for ten minutes. Add the flour and cook for a further minute, blend in the onion stock and seasoning, bring to the boil, cover and simmer for 15 to 20 minutes. Sieve or liquidize and return to the saucepan, add top of milk and heat gently. Serve with grated cheese.

ONION AND POTATO SOUP

Ingredients:

4 onions	2 medium potatoes
1½ pints vegetable stock	seasoning
½ pint milk	chopped chives

Method:

Peel and chop the onions and potatoes and cook in the stock till tender. Sieve or liquidize and return to the saucepan, add the milk and seasoning and gently heat. Serve with chopped chives.

MIXED VEGETABLE SOUP

Ingredients:

2 large onions	3 potatoes
2 carrots	1 stick celery
2 tomatoes	2 pints stock
corn oil	seasoning
chopped mint	

Method:

Prepare the vegetables and cut into small pieces. Heat the corn oil and simmer the onion for ten minutes, then add all the other vegetables and cook for five minutes while stirring. Add to the vegetable stock and simmer till all tender. Sieve or liquidize, return to the saucepan and heat. If required, one small carrot, one small onion and two oz peas can be chopped very small and cooked separately and added to the soup, after it has been liquidized and when the seasoning and chopped mint is added. Serve.

COUNTRY SOUP

Ingredients:

1 stick celery
2 carrots
1 oz rolled oats
1 dessertspoon yeast
extract

2 onions
1½ pints vegetable stock
seasoning
mixed chopped herbs

Method:

Wash and chop the celery, scrape and grate the carrots, peel and well chop the onions and place all in the stock in a saucepan. Bring to the boil, add the oats and extract and simmer for 15 minutes, season to taste and serve with chopped herbs.

CELERY SOUP

Ingredients:

1 stick celery
2 potatoes
¼ pint milk

2 onions
1½ pints vegetable stock
seasoning

Method:

Wash and cut the celery, peel and chop the onions, chop the potatoes, put in a saucepan with the stock and bring to the boil and simmer for about 30 minutes. Sieve or liquidize and return to saucepan, add the milk and seasoning and gently heat.

LENTIL SOUP

Ingredients:

2 large onions
2 pints vegetable stock
½ pint milk
seasoning

1 large carrot
1 stick celery
8 oz lentils
corn oil

Method:

Chop the vegetables roughly and cook in the corn oil, stirring for ten minutes. Stir in the stock, bring to the boil, add the washed lentils and simmer for 30 minutes. Add the milk and sieve or liquidize, return to the saucepan and heat gently.

VERMICELLI AND TOMATO SOUP

Ingredients:

14 oz tin tomatoes
1 pint vegetable stock
1 tablespoon tomato purée
seasoning

2 large onions
½ pint milk
4 oz vermicelli

Method:

Peel and chop the onions, put with the tomatoes in the stock in a saucepan and cook till tender. Sieve or liquidize and return to saucepan, add the purée and broken vermicelli and cook till tender. Add seasoning and milk, heat gently and serve.

CARROT SOUP

Ingredients:

2 large onions
2 pints vegetable stock
chopped chives

4 large carrots
top of milk

Method:

Peel and chop the onions, scrape and chop the carrots, put into the stock and cook till tender. Sieve or liquidize and return to saucepan, heat gently with the top of milk. Serve with chopped chives.

CHILLED LEEK SOUP

Ingredients:

1½ lb leeks
6 oz peeled tomatoes
1½ pints vegetable stock
2 potatoes
seasoning

corn oil
1 onion
1 pint milk
chopped chives

Method:

Wash and chop the leeks, peel and chop the onions, and cook in corn oil for 15 minutes. Add to the stock with the chopped potatoes and chopped tomatoes, simmer till tender. Sieve or liquidize and return to saucepan. Add the milk and seasoning and sprinkle with chopped chives. Chill and serve.

BROWN GRAVY

Ingredients:

½ pint vegetable stock	1 oz margarine
1 oz flour (wholemeal)	2 teaspoons yeast
seasoning	extract

Method:

Melt the margarine in a saucepan over a gentle heat. Add the flour and stir till lightly coloured. Add the stock slowly and simmer, stirring for five minutes. Add the extract and seasoning and stir until dissolved.

ITALIAN TOMATO SAUCE

Ingredients:

1 pint water	seasoning to taste
1 onion or 1 clove garlic	1 heaped tablespoon tomato
corn oil	purée
	1 dessertspoon wholemeal flour

Method:

Peel and chop the onion or garlic and cook in corn oil in the saucepan till tender. (If garlic, remove when brown.) Add the tomato purée and cook for five minutes. Add ¾ pint of water and simmer for about 30 minutes. Mix the flour with the remaining water, add to the mixture and bring to the boil and simmer for 15 minutes, adding the yeast extract.

ONION SAUCE

Ingredients:

½ pint vegetable stock   1 oz margarine
1 oz flour (wholemeal)   ½ teaspoon yeast extract
seasoning   1 medium onion

Method:

Peel and well chop the onion. Cook in the margarine till golden, stir in the flour and cook for a few minutes, stirring. Add the stock slowly and simmer, stirring, for five minutes. Add the extract and seasoning and stir until well mixed.

WHITE SAUCE

Ingredients:

1 oz margarine   ½ pint milk
1 oz flour (wholemeal)   seasoning

Method:

Melt the margarine in a saucepan over a gentle heat. Add the flour and stir continuously for two minutes. Gradually stir in the milk and simmer, stirring, for five to eight minutes. Add the seasoning and an extra ¼ oz margarine for a creamy sauce.

HERB WHITE SAUCE

Ingredients:

1 oz margarine	½ pint milk
1 oz flour (wholemeal)	2 teaspoons chopped mint,
seasoning	parsley or mixed herbs

Method:

Melt the margarine in a saucepan over a gentle heat. Add the flour and stir continuously for two minutes. Gradually stir in the milk and simmer, stirring, for five to eight minutes. Add the herbs and seasoning and stir well.

CHEESE SAUCE

Ingredients:

1 oz margarine	½ pint milk
1 oz flour (wholemeal)	3 oz grated cheese
seasoning	

Method:

Melt the margarine in a saucepan over a gentle heat. Add the flour and stir continuously for two minutes. Gradually stir in the milk and simmer, stirring, for five to eight minutes. Add the grated cheese and seasoning and stir until dissolved.

CHEESE, EGG AND VEGETABLE SAVOURIES

TOMATO ROAST

Ingredients:

6 oz grated Cheddar cheese	4 oz tomatoes
2 onions	4 oz fresh brown breadcrumbs
2 eggs	1 teaspoon chopped parsley
seasoning	1 teaspoon yeast extract
corn oil	

Method:

Peel and chop the onions and fry in corn oil till tender and golden. Skin and chop the tomatoes. Mix the breadcrumbs with the grated cheese, onions and tomatoes, seasoning, extract and beaten eggs. Put in a greased baking dish.

Bake in oven set at 400 deg F (Mark 6) for 30-45 minutes.

TOMATO AND OAT ROAST

Ingredients:

1 large onion	2 oz rolled oats
4 oz tomatoes	2 oz fresh brown breadcrumbs
1 teaspoon yeast extract	2 eggs
1 teaspoon mixed herbs	seasoning
corn oil	4 oz grated cheese

Method:

Peel and chop the onion and cook in corn oil till tender. Skin the tomatoes and cut into pieces, mix with the cooked onion. Mix the breadcrumbs, oats, extract, herbs, seasoning and grated cheese with the beaten eggs, onion and tomatoes. Put in a greased baking dish.

Bake in oven set at 400 deg F (Mark 6) for 35-45 minutes.

TOMATO AND OAT SAVOURY

Ingredients:

3-4 oz rolled oats
8 oz grated Cheddar cheese
14 oz tin tomatoes

½ small cup of milk flavoured
with 1 teaspoon yeast
extract

Method:

Grease a baking dish and sprinkle half the oats on the bottom. Follow this with 4½ oz grated cheese. Put on the tin of tomatoes and cut in halves. Follow with the remaining oats and top all with the remaining grated cheese. Press down and pour over the milk and extract. Put in the oven.
Bake in oven set at 425 deg F (Mark 7) for 40-45 minutes until golden brown. Allow to stand out of the oven for five minutes before serving.

ONION AND OAT SAVOURY

Ingredients:

6 oz grated Cheddar cheese
3 oz rolled oats
½ teaspoon mixed herbs
corn oil

2 large onions
2 eggs
1 teaspoon yeast extract
seasoning to taste

Method:

Peel and chop the onions and fry in corn oil till brown. Beat the eggs. Mix the fried onions with the oats, grated cheese, beaten eggs, seasoning, mixed herbs and yeast extract. Put in a greased oven-proof dish.
Bake for 45 minutes or until set and lightly browned. Oven set at 400 deg F (Mark 6).

ONION AND WHEAT SAVOURY

Ingredients:

4 Shredded Wheat sections	6 oz grated Cheddar cheese
4 medium onions	½ cup of milk
seasoning to taste	1 teaspoon yeast extract

Method:

Grease a baking dish with margarine. Peel and roughly chop the onions and boil in water till tender. Crumble two of the Shredded Wheat sections into the baking dish, then 3 oz of the grated cheese followed by the boiled and drained onions. Top these with the remaining two crumbled Shredded Wheat sections and, finally, with the 3 oz grated cheese. Press down firmly. Mix the seasoning with the milk and yeast extract and pour over the top of the savoury.

Bake for 40-50 minutes or until golden brown. Oven set at 400 deg F (Mark 6).

TOMATO AND CHEESE BAKE

Ingredients:

4 oz wholemeal s/r flour	¼ pint milk
2 eggs	½ level teaspoon salt
6 oz grated Cheddar cheese	6 oz fresh tomatoes
chopped chives or onion tops	

Method:

Skin the tomatoes and cut in half; place in a greased baking dish and sprinkle with the chopped chives. Mix the flour, eggs, salt and milk to a batter and add the grated cheese. Pour over the tomatoes and bake.

Bake in oven set at 400 deg F (Mark 6) for 35-40 minutes.

MUSHROOM AND ONION ROAST

Ingredients:

4-6 oz grated Cheddar cheese	4 oz mushrooms
2 onions	4 oz fresh brown breadcrumbs
2 eggs	1 teaspoon mixed herbs
seasoning	1 teaspoon yeast extract
corn oil	

Method:

Peel and chop the onions and fry in corn oil till tender and golden. Wash the mushrooms and chop roughly, adding to the onions in the last five minutes of cooking. Mix the breadcrumbs with the grated cheese, onions and mushrooms, seasoning, extract and beaten eggs. Put in a greased baking dish.

Bake in oven set at 400 deg F (Mark 6) for 35-45 minutes.

MUSHROOM AND ONION BAKE

Ingredients:

4 oz wholemeal s/r flour	2 eggs
¼ pint milk	4-6 oz grated Cheddar cheese
1 onion	4 oz mushrooms
seasoning	corn oil

Method:

Peel and chop the onion and fry in corn oil till golden, adding the washed and roughly chopped mushrooms in the last five minutes of cooking. Make a batter with the flour, eggs, milk and seasoning and add the grated cheese. Place the onion and mushrooms in the greased baking dish and pour over the cheese batter.

Bake in oven set at 400 deg F (Mark 6) for 35-45 minutes.

MUSHROOM AND CELERY SAVOURY

Ingredients:

4 oz mushrooms	1 stick celery
6 oz grated Cheddar cheese	3 oz fresh brown breadcrumbs
2 eggs	corn oil
seasoning	1 teaspoon mixed herbs
	(optional)

Method:

Wash and chop the celery and boil in water till tender. Drain well. Wash the mushrooms, chop roughly, and fry in corn oil for five minutes. Mix the celery with the mushrooms and cheese, mix in the crumbled breadcrumbs and beaten eggs with seasoning and herbs. Put into a greased baking dish.

Bake for 45 minutes. Oven set at 400 deg F (Mark 6).

ONION RISSOLES

Ingredients:

4 oz grated Cheddar cheese	2 medium onions
1 medium carrot (3 oz weight)	4 oz Mapleton's Frittamix
2 eggs	or equivalent
1 teaspoon mixed herbs	¼ teaspoon curry powder
corn oil	golden breadcrumbs

Method:

Peel and chop the onions and fry in corn oil till golden. Grate the carrot very fine, and mix this with the grated cheese, Frittamix, herbs, fried onions and beaten eggs. Mix thoroughly and allow to cool. Form into rissoles and roll in the golden breadcrumbs. Heat a baking tray with corn oil and place the rissoles on it.

Bake in oven set at 425 deg (Mark 7) for 30 minutes. Turn at 15 minutes.

CHEESE AND EGG SAVOURIES

Ingredients:

8 oz shortcrust pastry

8 oz wholemeal s/r flour	4 oz margarine
water to mix	¼ teaspoon salt

Filling

6 oz Cheddar cheese	5 tomatoes
4 hard boiled eggs	1 teaspoon herbs
seasoning	top of milk or beaten egg

Method:

Roll out the pastry and cut into large rounds. Dice the cheese. Skin and chop the tomatoes. Chop the eggs. Blend all together with herbs and seasoning. Put piles of the mixture on to the centre of each round of pastry, brush the edges with water and seal together. Lift on to lightly greased baking sheet and brush the tops with milk or beaten egg.

Bake in oven set at 425 deg F (Mark 7) for 20-25 minutes.

CHEESE AND CORN SAVOURY

Ingredients:

2 oz corn flakes	6 oz grated Cheddar cheese
4 eggs	½ pint milk
seasoning	1 teaspoon mixed herbs

Method:

Beat the eggs in the milk with the seasoning and herbs. Mix the cheese and corn flakes together and put in a greased baking dish. Pour over it the milk and egg mixture.

Bake in oven set at 400 deg F (Mark 6) for 35-45 minutes or until golden and set.

TOMATO FLAN

Ingredients:

6 oz shortcrust pastry
6 oz wholemeal s/r flour
water to mix

3 oz margarine
¼ teaspoon salt

Filling
6 oz grated Cheddar cheese
just under ¼ pint milk
seasoning

2 eggs
6 large tomatoes
chopped chives or parsley

Method:

Mix the pastry to dough and roll out into a seven-eight inch flan dish. Put half the grated cheese on the pastry followed by the skinned and chopped tomatoes with either the chopped parsley or chives. Top this with the remaining grated cheese. Pour on the beaten eggs mixed with the milk and seasoning.

Bake in oven set at 400 deg F (Mark 6) for 35-45 minutes, till set.

ONION FLAN

Ingredients:

Pastry
4 oz wholemeal s/r flour
water to mix

2 oz margarine

Filling
2 large onions
corn oil

2 eggs
8 oz grated Cheddar cheese

Method:

Make up the pastry and roll out to line a flan case. Peel and chop the onions and fry in corn oil till golden.

Separate the egg whites from the yolks and whisk the whites till stiff. Fold into the whites 3 oz of cheese. Mix together the onions, egg yolks and 4 oz grated cheese and place in the pastry case. Put the egg whites and cheese mixture on top, and sprinkle with the remaining cheese.

Bake in oven set at 425 deg F (Mark 7) for 35-45 minutes or till the pastry is cooked and the top of the mixture golden.

MUSHROOM FLAN

Ingredients:

6 oz shortcrust pastry with cheese

6 oz wholemeal s/r flour	2 oz margarine
1½ oz grated Cheddar cheese	¼ teaspoon salt
water to mix	

Filling

2 onions	4 oz mushrooms
just under ¼ pint milk	2 eggs
corn oil	4 oz grated cheese
seasoning	

Method:

Peel and chop the onions and cook in corn oil till golden. Add the washed and roughly chopped mushrooms in the last five minutes of cooking. Beat the eggs with the milk and seasoning. Mix the grated cheese with the onions and mushrooms and put in the flan case, pour over the egg and milk mixture.

Bake in oven 400 deg F (Mark 6) for 35-45 minutes or till set.

SWEET CORN FLAN

Ingredients:

> *6 oz shortcrust pastry*
> 6 oz wholemeal s/r flour   3 oz margarine
> water to mix   ¼ teaspoon salt
>
> *Filling*
> 4 oz grated Cheddar cheese   11½ oz tin sweet corn
> just under ¼ pint milk   2 eggs
> seasoning

Method:

Mix the pastry and roll out into a seven-eight inch flan dish. Mix the sweet corn and grated cheese together and place on the pastry. Beat the eggs with the milk and seasoning, and pour over the cheese and sweet corn.

Bake in oven set at 400 deg F (Mark 6) for 35-45 minutes, till set.

GOLDEN ONION FLAN

Ingredients:

> *6 oz shortcrust pastry*
> 6 oz wholemeal s/r flour   3 oz margarine
> water to mix   ¼ teaspoon salt
>
> *Filling*
> 2 onions   ¼ pint milk (just under)
> 5 oz grated Cheddar cheese   1 large egg
> seasoning

Method:

Roll pastry into an eight inch sandwich tin, pinching the edges. Peel and slice the onions and boil in water till tender, drain well. Blend in 3 oz grated cheese together with the beaten egg, milk and seasoning. Mix in the onions and pour into the pastry case. Sprinkle with the remaining cheese.

Bake in oven set at 425 deg F (Mark 7) for 10 minutes, reducing to 400 deg F (Mark 6) for 25-30 minutes, till golden and set.

VEGETABLE PIE

Ingredients:

Pie lid

4 oz wholemeal s/r flour	2½ oz margarine
water to mix	½ teaspoon salt

Filling

1 stick celery	2 onions
4 tomatoes	2 carrots
½ pint vegetable stock	1 teaspoon yeast extract
1 teaspoon flour	corn oil
6 oz grated Cheddar cheese	1 beaten egg

Method:

Wash and chop the celery. Peel and chop the onions and fry both in corn oil until tender. Add the flour and the stock, stirring. Add the sliced carrots and skinned and chopped tomatoes and bring to the boil. Add the yeast extract and place in a casserole; cook in oven set at 425 deg F (Mark 7) for 25 minutes. Make up the pastry and roll out to fit the casserole dish. Bring the vegetables out of the oven and put the grated cheese on top, cap this with the pastry lid, pinch the edges and brush with a beaten egg. Return to the oven for further 25-30 minutes.

ONION AND CHEESE PIE

Ingredients:

8 oz shortcrust pastry

8 oz wholemeal s/r flour	4 oz margarine
water to mix	½ teaspoon salt

Filling

2 large Spanish onions	8 oz grated cheese
top of milk or beaten egg	

Method:

Make the pastry by rubbing the margarine into the flour and salt, and adding water to make a dough. Roll out the pastry and line the pie dish with half. Roll the remaining half for the pie lid. Peel and chop the onions and boil in water till tender. Put a layer of grated cheese on the pastry and then half the drained onions. Follow with more cheese and the remainder of the onions and top with grated cheese. Put the pastry lid on the pie, pinching the edges firmly, and trim. Make a slit in the middle and brush over with top of milk or beaten egg. Bake for 45 minutes in oven set at 425 deg F (Mark 7).

MUSHROOM AND CHEESE PIE

Ingredients:

Shortcrust pastry

8 oz wholemeal s/r flour	4 oz margarine
water to mix	½ teaspoon salt

Filling

1 large onion	4 oz mushrooms
4 large tomatoes	8 oz grated Cheddar cheese
1 beaten egg to glaze	corn oil

Method:

Make up the pastry. Cut in half and roll out both pieces to fit the pie dish. Place the bottom half in the pie dish.

Peel and chop the onion. Wash and chop the mush-rooms. Skin and chop the tomatoes. Cook the onion in the corn oil until tender, adding the mushrooms and tomatoes in last five minutes of cooking. Put a layer of grated cheese in the pastry, follow by half the onion mixture, a second layer of cheese, again the onion mix-ture and top with the remaining cheese. Place the pastry lid on, seal the edges firmly. Brush with the beaten egg. Bake in oven set at 400 deg F (Mark 6) for 35-45 minutes.

COVERED PIZZA PIE

Ingredients:

12 oz shortcrust pastry
12 oz wholemeal s/r flour   6 oz margarine
water to mix

Filling
8 oz grated cheese   3 medium onions
2 hard boiled eggs   4 tomatoes (fresh)
corn oil   1 egg (beaten) or top of milk
    for glaze

Method:

Roll out half the pastry and line an eight inch round shallow dish. Place on it half the cheese. Peel, chop and fry the onions in corn oil till golden and place on top of the cheese. Cut each egg into six slices and lay on the cheese, yolk down. Cover with thinly sliced and skinned tomatoes; add the remaining cheese. Roll out the remaining pastry and cover the pie, pinch the edges and brush with the beaten egg or milk.

Bake in oven set at 400 deg F (Mark 6) for 20-30 minutes.

OPEN PIZZA PIE

Ingredients:

6 oz *shortcrust pastry*
6 oz wholemeal s/r flour   3 oz margarine
water to mix

Filling
4 fresh tomatoes   4 oz mushrooms
1 small chopped raw onion   4 oz cubed cheese
corn oil   seasoning

Method:

Roll out the pastry and line an eight inch round shallow dish. Skin the tomatoes and slice and put on the pastry, followed by the chopped onion. Put on the cubed cheese and top with the mushrooms and seasoning. Pour over one large teaspoon of corn oil and press down.
Bake in oven set at 400 deg F (Mark 6) for 15-20 minutes.

SWEET CORN FRITTERS

Ingredients:

11½ oz tin of sweet corn   ¼ pint milk (just under)
4 oz wholemeal s/r flour   1 egg
seasoning   pinch of mixed herbs
corn oil

Method:

Mix the flour and seasoning. Beat the eggs in the milk, mix with the flour and make a batter. Stir in the drained sweet corn and herbs. Place tablespoonsful of this mixture into a frying pan of well-heated corn oil (quite shallow). Turn when the underside is cooked and golden, and cook the second side.

STUFFED TOMATOES

Ingredients:

4 large tomatoes	1 small grated onion
2 oz fresh brown breadcrumbs	1 egg
2 teaspoons chopped parsley	2 oz ground cashew nuts
margarine	1 teaspoon chopped mint
	seasoning

Method:

Wash the tomatoes and cut off a small lid. Remove the insides and mix with the breadcrumbs, nuts, onion and herbs with the beaten egg and seasoning. Place the mixture in each tomato, put the lid on and dot with margarine. Place on a greased baking tray and cover with greased paper.

Bake in oven set at 400 deg F (Mark 6) for 15-20 minutes.

STUFFED ONIONS

Ingredients:

4 large onions	seasoning
4 oz grated carrots	4 oz grated cheese
1 egg	2 oz fresh brown breadcrumbs
	1 teaspoon sage

Method:

Peel the onions and cook gently in water for 30 minutes. Remove from the water and carefully remove the centres. Mix the onion centres with the grated carrots, grated cheese, breadcrumbs, sage, seasoning and beaten egg. Fill the onion cases with the mixture and put on greased dish.

Bake in oven set at 400 deg F (Mark 6) for 30 minutes.

TOMATO STUFFED MARROW

Ingredients:

1 medium marrow	1 heaped teaspoon sage
2 onions	2 eggs
3 oz fresh brown breadcrumbs	4 large tomatoes
3 oz crumbled Shredded Wheat	½ red or green pepper
	corn oil
	1 teaspoon yeast extract

Method:

Peel and chop the onions and fry in corn oil until golden, with the washed and well-chopped pepper. Skin and chop the tomatoes. Beat the eggs. Mix all the ingredients together. Wash the marrow. Peel only if tough. Cut in half and scoop out the seeds. Place one half on a greased baking tray and fill with the tomato stuffing, place the remaining half of the marrow on top and dot with margarine.

Bake in oven set at 425 deg F (Mark 7) for 45-50 minutes, or till tender.

STUFFED MUSHROOM OR TOMATO ROLLS

Ingredients:

Cheese pastry

8 oz wholemeal s/r flour	3 oz margarine
2 oz grated cheese	water to mix
1 beaten egg for glaze	

Stuffing

For the stuffing use either the mushroom or the tomato stuffing as for the stuffed marrow.

Method:

Mix the pastry, cut in half and roll into oblongs three inches wide and fairly thin. Place the filling down the

centre of one piece of pastry. Brush the pastry edges with water and place the second pastry oblong on top, pinch the edges well together and cutting them off as close as possible. Brush with the beaten egg and cut into two inch rolls. Place on a baking tray.
Bake in oven set at 425 deg F (Mark 7) for 30-40 minutes.

MUSHROOM STUFFED MARROW

Ingredients:

1 medium marrow	4 oz grated Cheddar cheese
4-6 oz mushrooms	2 onions
2 eggs	1 teaspoon sage
1 teaspoon mixed herbs	2 oz rissole powder
corn oil	1 teaspoon yeast extract

Method:

Peel and chop the onions and fry in the corn oil until golden. Wash and roughly chop the mushrooms and add for the last five minutes of cooking. Mix the rissole powder, beaten eggs, herbs, grated cheese, extract and onions and mushrooms well together. Wash the marrow. Peel only if tough. Cut in half and scoop out the seeds. Put on a greased baking tray and pile the mushroom stuffing in the scooped-out centre, place the remaining half of the marrow on top, and dot with margarine.
Bake in oven set at 425 deg F (Mark 7) for 45-50 minutes, till tender.

POTATO AND ONION CASSEROLE

Ingredients:

1 lb potatoes	2 large onions
½ lb tomatoes	seasoning
1 teaspoon herbs	4 oz margarine
Sauce	
1 oz margarine	1 oz wholemeal flour
½ pint milk	4 oz grated cheese

Method:

Peel and slice the onions. Slice the potatoes. Skin and slice the tomatoes. Place all in layers in a greased baking dish. Put on the herbs and seasoning and dot with margarine. Cover and cook in oven 375 deg F (Mark 5) for 50-60 minutes, till tender. Make up the cheese sauce. Remove the dish from the oven and pour the sauce over; return to the oven for a further 15 minutes till golden.

ONION CASSEROLE

Ingredients:

2 large onions	1 oz margarine
4 hard-boiled eggs	
Sauce	
1½ oz margarine	1½ oz wholemeal flour
¾ pint milk	4 oz grated Cheddar cheese
seasoning	½ pepper

Method:

Wash and finely chop the pepper. Peel and slice the onions and fry in margarine till pale gold, with the pepper. Place in a greased casserole dish and arrange

sliced hard-boiled eggs over the top. Cover with the cheese sauce. To make the sauce, melt the margarine in saucepan, stir in the flour and cook gently, blending in the milk to form a smooth sauce. Bring to the boil and simmer for three minutes, stirring well, then blend in the grated cheese and seasoning.
Bake for 35 minutes till golden brown. Oven set at 400 deg F (Mark 6).

TOMATO AND CELERY CASSEROLE

Ingredients:

4 oz mushrooms	4 tomatoes
2 large onions	2 pieces celery
2 teaspoons herbs	½ small pepper
1 dessertspoon yeast extract	2 hard-boiled eggs
1 teaspoon curry powder	just under ¼ pint stock
corn oil	grated cheese

Method:

Peel and chop the onions. Wash and chop the celery. Cook both in corn oil till tender. Skin the tomatoes and chop. Wash and roughly chop the mushrooms. Quarter the eggs. Grease a casserole and place in layers the onion and celery, eggs, mushrooms and tomatoes. Mix the extract with the stock, herbs and curry powder and pour it over the vegetables. Serve with grated cheese.
Bake in oven set at 400 deg F (Mark 6) for 40-45 minutes.

TOMATO AND MUSHROOM CASSEROLE

Ingredients:

8 oz mushrooms
3 onions
1 tablespoon chopped parsley
just under ¼ pint vegetable
    stock

4 tomatoes
1 teaspoon yeast extract
corn oil
grated cheese

Method:

Peel and chop the onions. Skin and chop the tomatoes. Wash and chop the mushrooms. Cook the onions in corn oil until tender, adding the mushrooms and tomatoes in the last five minutes of cooking. Place in a greased casserole. Dissolve the extract in the vegetable stock and mix in the parsley. Pour over the vegetables. Bake in oven set at 400 deg F (Mark 6) for 20-25 minutes. Serve with grated cheese.

LENTIL CASSEROLE

Ingredients:

1 small pepper (optional)
2 large onions
8 oz lentils
2 pints vegetable stock
seasoning
grated cheese

2 large carrots
1 stick celery
½ pint milk
1 dessertspoon yeast extract
corn oil

Method:

Chop the vegetables roughly and cook in corn oil for ten minutes. Stir in the stock and bring to the boil. Add the washed lentils. Simmer for about 30 minutes and add the extract and seasoning. Add the milk and bring nearly to the boil again. Serve with grated cheese.

VEGETABLE CASSEROLE

Ingredients:

2 lb potatoes	1 large turnip
4 pieces celery	$\frac{1}{2}$ lb carrots
1 lb leeks	1 large onion
corn oil	14 oz can tomatoes
grated cheese	seasoning
1 dessertspoon yeast extract	

Method:

Slice the potatoes, scrub the celery, peel and cut the turnip and carrots into dice. Wash the leeks and chop. Peel and chop the onion. Put the potatoes and celery into a pan with some corn oil, add the carrots, turnip, leeks and onion and cook all for ten minutes, stirring with the yeast extract. Season and put in a greased casserole and top with the tomatoes. Cover and bake in oven set at 335 deg F (Mark 3) for 2-2$\frac{1}{2}$ hours till tender. Serve with grated cheese.

MUSHROOM TARTS

Ingredients:

4 oz shortcrust pastry	
4 oz wholemeal s/r flour	2 oz margarine
water to mix	
Filling	
4 oz mushrooms	4 oz grated Cheddar cheese
2 tablespoons white sauce	seasoning
corn oil	

[See overleaf for method

Method:

Mix the pastry and roll out. Cut with three inch cutter and place in 12 deep patty tins. Wash and chop the mushrooms and cook in corn oil for five minutes. Add the mushrooms to the white sauce and grated cheese and seasoning. Place spoonsful on the pastry cases.
Bake in oven set at 425 deg F (Mark 7) for 20-25 minutes.

VEGETABLE ROLL

Ingredients:

8 oz shortcrust pastry
8 oz wholemeal s/r flour	4 oz margarine
water to mix	¼ teaspoon salt

Filling
2 onions	1 teaspoon yeast extract
½ medium cabbage	1 teaspoon mixed herbs
4 oz mushrooms	2 large tomatoes
corn oil	

Method:

Roll out the pastry into an oblong. Peel and chop the onions and wash and well chop the cabbage. Wash and roughly chop the mushrooms. Skin and chop the tomatoes. Cook all in corn oil till tender, mix with the herbs and extract. Spread the mixture down the pastry and press moistened edges together. Brush with beaten egg. Place on a baking sheet.
Bake in oven set at 425 deg F (Mark 7) for 40 minutes.

SWEET CORN CHOWDER

Ingredients:

½ lb potatoes	¼ pint top of milk
1 green pepper	14 oz tin tomatoes
3 large onions	11 oz tin sweet corn
seasoning	1 large teaspoon yeast
grated cheese	extract

Method:

Cut the potatoes into cubes. Wash the pepper and remove the seeds and chop. Peel and chop the onions. Place the vegetables in a pan and add the tomatoes, sweet corn, seasoning and yeast extract. Bring to the boil, cover and simmer for 45-60 minutes till tender. Blend in the milk before serving. Serve with grated cheese.

CHEESE SOUFFLE

Ingredients:

3 eggs	¼ pint milk
1 oz margarine	½ oz wholemeal flour
4 oz grated Cheddar cheese	seasoning

Method:

Separate the egg yolks from the whites. Melt the margarine in a saucepan and stir in the flour; add the milk gradually, stirring well until boiling. Cool slightly and add the egg yolks; beat well. Season and add the grated cheese to the mixture. Whisk the egg whites and gently fold into the cheese mixture. Pour into a well greased soufflé dish.

Bake in oven set at 400 deg F (Mark 6) for 30-40 minutes.

RICE, LENTIL AND MILLOTTO SAVOURIES

MUSHROOM AND LENTIL SAVOURY

Ingredients:

4 oz lentils	2 onions
4 oz grated Cheddar cheese	1 teaspoon chopped parsley
1 teaspoon yeast extract	2 eggs
4 oz mushrooms	corn oil

Method:

Cook the lentils till tender in sufficient boiling water; drain any excess moisture. Peel and chop the onions and fry in corn oil till golden, adding the washed and roughly chopped mushrooms in the last five minutes of cooking. Beat the eggs and mix all the ingredients together and put in a greased baking dish.

Bake in oven set at 400 deg F (Mark 6) for 35-45 minutes.

LENTIL ROAST

Ingredients:

4 oz lentils	3 oz grated Cheddar cheese
2 eggs	1 oz fresh brown breadcrumbs
2 onions	1 dessertspoon chopped
seasoning	parsley
	corn oil

Method:

Cook the lentils in sufficient boiling water until tender. Drain any excess moisture. Peel and chop the onion and fry in corn oil until golden. Mix the lentils, grated cheese, onion, breadcrumbs, seasoning and parsley together. Place in a greased baking dish.

Bake in oven set at 400 deg F (Mark 6) for 35-45 minutes.

TOMATO AND LENTIL SAVOURY

Ingredients:

4 oz lentils	6 oz fresh tomatoes
1 onion	4 oz grated Cheddar cheese
2 eggs	1 teaspoon yeast extract
1 teaspoon chopped mint	corn oil

Method:

Cook the lentils until tender in just sufficient boiling water. Drain any excess moisture. Peel and chop the onion and fry in corn oil until golden. Skin the tomatoes by soaking quickly in boiling water, and chop roughly. Beat the eggs and mix with the lentils, onion, grated cheese, extract, chopped mint and tomatoes. Put into a greased baking dish.

Bake in oven set at 400 deg F (Mark 6) for 35-45 minutes.

ONION AND LENTIL ROAST

Ingredients:

4 oz lentils	2 onions
5 oz grated Cheddar cheese	2 eggs
seasoning	1 teaspoon yeast extract

Method:

Peel and chop the onions, wash the lentils and put both in sufficient boiling water till cooked and water absorbed; if any excess water drain well. Mix in the grated cheese, beaten eggs, seasoning and yeast extract. Put in a greased baking dish.

Bake in oven set at 400 deg F (Mark 6) for 35-45 minutes, or until set and golden.

LENTIL RISSOLES

Ingredients:

6 oz lentils	corn oil
2 medium onions	2 oz grated cheese
1 egg	2 oz fresh brown breadcrumbs
golden breadcrumbs	1 teaspoon mixed herbs
	seasoning

Method:

Peel, chop and fry the onions in corn oil till tender and golden. Boil the lentils in sufficient boiling water till tender. Drain well any excess moisture. Mix all ingredients together and cool. Form the cold mixture into rissoles and roll well in the breadcrumbs.

Bake in oven set at 425 deg F (Mark 7) on a well-heated baking tray just covered with corn oil. Turn over the rissoles at 15 minutes and cook for further 15 minutes.

CHEESE AND LENTIL BAKE

Ingredients:

4 oz lentils	2 onions
6 oz grated Cheddar cheese	2 eggs
1 teaspoon yeast extract	corn oil
seasoning	2 tomatoes (optional)

Method:

Peel and chop the onions and cook in corn oil till golden. Cook the lentils in sufficient boiling water till tender; drain any excess moisture. Mix the lentils with the onions, grated cheese, beaten eggs, seasoning and yeast extract. Put in a greased baking dish. Arrange on top the skinned and thinly sliced tomatoes.

Bake in oven 400 deg F (Mark 6) for 30-45 minutes.

SHREDDED WHEAT AND LENTIL SAVOURY

Ingredients:

4 oz lentils	2 eggs
2 Shredded Wheat sections	4 oz tomatoes (fresh)
5 oz grated Cheddar cheese	2 onions
corn oil	seasoning

Method:

Wash the lentils and cook in boiling water till tender; drain any excess moisture. Peel and chop the onions and fry in corn oil till tender and golden. Skin the tomatoes and roughly chop. Crumble the Shredded Wheat sections and mix with the grated cheese. Put by a cupful for topping. Mix the ingredients all together and put in a greased baking dish. Put the remaining wheat and cheese mixture on top, and dot with margarine.

Bake in oven set at 400 deg F (Mark 6) for 35-45 minutes.

CHEESE MILLOTTO SAVOURY

Ingredients:

4 oz Millotto	1 teaspoon mixed herbs
4-6 oz grated Cheddar cheese	2 onions
seasoning	2 eggs
	1 teaspoon yeast extract

Method:

Peel and chop the onions and boil in water with the Millotto till the water is absorbed and the onions tender. Beat the eggs and add, with the grated cheese, extract, seasoning and herbs, to the Millotto and onions and mix well. Place in a greased baking dish.

Bake in oven set at 400 deg F (Mark 6) for 30-35 minutes.

49

D

MUSHROOM AND MILLOTTO SAVOURY

Ingredients:

4 oz Millotto	1 onion
4 oz mushrooms	4 oz grated cheese
2 eggs	corn oil
seasoning	1 teaspoon herbs

Method:

Put the Millotto in boiling water and cook till tender and the water absorbed. Peel and chop the onion and cook in corn oil till golden, adding the washed and roughly chopped mushrooms in the last five minutes of cooking. Well mix the cooked Millotto with the cooked onion and mushrooms, grated cheese, seasoning, herbs and beaten eggs. Place in a greased baking dish.

Bake in oven set at 400 deg F (Mark 6) for 30-35 minutes.

TOMATO AND MILLOTTO SAVOURY

Ingredients:

4 oz Millotto	3 tomatoes
6 oz grated Cheddar cheese	2 eggs
seasoning	1 teaspoon chopped parsley
1 teaspoon yeast extract	

Method:

Put the Millotto in boiling water and cook till the water is absorbed and the Millotto tender. Skin the tomatoes and chop. Beat the eggs. Mix the grated cheese, chopped tomatoes, beaten eggs, seasoning, yeast extract and chopped parsley with the Millotto and place in a greased baking dish.

Bake in oven set at 400 deg F (Mark 6) for 30-35 minutes.

MILLOTTO RISSOLES

Ingredients:

4 oz Millotto	corn oil
1 teaspoon yeast extract	2 onions
4 oz cheese (optional)	just over ½ pint water
golden breadcrumbs	1 egg
	herbs to taste

Method:

Peel and chop the onions and add with the Millotto to the water and extract; bring to the boil and simmer for ten minutes, till tender and water absorbed. Cool. Grate the cheese and beat the egg and add to the Millotto and onions, with herbs, and mix well. When cool, form into rissoles and roll well in the breadcrumbs. Place on a baking tray with heated corn oil for 20 minutes, turning at 15 minutes and cooking for a further five minutes.

Bake in oven set at 400 deg F (Mark 6).

TOMATO RICE

Ingredients:

3 oz brown rice	8 oz fresh tomatoes
6 oz grated Cheddar cheese	2 eggs
seasoning	1 teaspoon chopped parsley

Method:

Wash and cook the rice till tender in boiling water. Skin and chop the tomatoes. Mix the cooked rice with the grated cheese, tomatoes, beaten eggs, chopped parsley and seasoning. Place in a greased baking dish.

Bake in an oven set at 400 deg F (Mark 6) for 30-40 minutes.

CHEESE AND ONION RICE

Ingredients:

3 oz brown rice	2 large onions
6 oz grated Cheddar cheese	2 eggs
seasoning	1 teaspoon yeast extract

Method:

Wash the rice and boil in water together with the peeled and chopped onions until both are tender. Mix the cooked rice and onions with the beaten eggs, grated cheese, yeast extract and seasoning. Place in a greased baking dish.

Bake in oven set at 400 deg F (Mark 6) for 30-40 minutes.

RICE CROQUETTES

Ingredients:

3 oz brown rice	1 large onion
3 oz grated Cheddar cheese	1 oz fresh brown breadcrumbs
$\frac{1}{2}$ teaspoon curry powder	seasoning
corn oil	golden breadcrumbs

Method:

Peel and chop the onion and fry in corn oil till golden. Wash the rice and cook in boiling water till tender. Mix the rice with the onion, breadcrumbs, grated cheese, curry powder and seasoning. Cool. Form into croquettes and roll in the golden breadcrumbs. Cover a baking tray with corn oil and heat. Place the croquettes on.

Bake in oven set at 425 deg F (Mark 7) for 30 minutes. Turn at 15 minutes.

RICE AND MUSHROOM CURRY

Ingredients:

4 oz brown rice	2 large onions
4-6 oz mushrooms	1 small pepper
¼ pint vegetable stock	3 oz wholemeal flour
1 dessertspoon lemon juice	2 teaspoons curry powder
1 oz raisins	corn oil

Method:

Wash the rice and cook until tender. Peel and chop the onions, wash and well-chop the pepper, and fry both in corn oil till tender. Wash the mushrooms and roughly chop; add to the onions and pepper in the last five minutes of cooking. When cooked, mix-in the flour and curry powder and gently cook for five minutes, stirring. Add the stock and lemon juice. Mix well and add the raisins and cook slowly for 15 minutes. Pile the rice on a serving dish and put the curry sauce on top.

VEGETABLE CURRY

Ingredients:

½ lb cooked mixed vegetables	4 oz brown rice
1 chopped onion	1 small chopped apple
1 oz wholemeal flour	corn oil
1 oz curry powder	½ oz brown sugar
1 teaspoon lemon juice	1 oz raisins
½ teaspoon salt	½ pint vegetable stock

Method:

Cook the washed rice in boiling water unitl tender. Cook the onion in corn oil till golden, add the flour and curry powder, mix and gradually add the stock and salt. Cook for a few minutes, add the remaining ingredients and simmer for 15 minutes. Place the cooked rice on a serving dish and pile the vegetable curry on top.

RISOTTO

Ingredients:

3 oz brown rice	2 onions
4 oz mushrooms	1 small packet frozen peas
8 oz tomatoes	1 small green pepper
1 tin (5 oz) tomato purée	seasoning
½ teaspoon curry powder	corn oil
little vegetable stock	

Method:

Wash and cook the rice in water until tender. Peel and chop the onions and fry in corn oil with the washed and well-chopped pepper till tender. Wash and roughly chop the mushrooms and add to the onions and pepper in the last five minutes of cooking. Skin and chop the tomatoes and add to the cooked onion, mushroom and pepper. Cook the frozen peas quickly. Mix the rice, onions, mushrooms, pepper and tomatoes with the peas and tomato purée, add the curry powder, stock and seasoning. This can be heated in the saucepan while stirring, or put in an oven-proof dish for 20-30 minutes, in a moderate oven.

VEGETABLE RISOTTO

Ingredients:

4 oz brown rice	1 onion
1 carrot	1 piece celery
2 tomatoes	1 teaspoon yeast extract
1 tablespoon chopped parsley	seasoning
¼ pint water	1 tin (5 oz) tomato purée
2 oz mushrooms	corn oil
grated cheese	

Method:

Peel and chop the onion. Wash and chop the celery. Skin and chop the tomatoes. Wash and chop the mushrooms. Scrape the carrot and chop. Heat corn oil in saucepan and put in all the vegetables for five minutes, cooking while stirring. Add the washed rice and cook for few minutes. Add the boiled water, seasoning and extract and cook till rice is tender and water absorbed. Stir in the tomato purée and parsley. Serve with grated cheese.

STUFFED GREEN PEPPERS

Ingredients:

4 green peppers	1 large onion
4 oz grated Cheddar cheese	4 oz mushrooms
corn oil	4 tomatoes
3 oz brown rice	1 teaspoon mixed herbs
seasoning	1 egg

Method:

Wash the peppers and cut off the tops, remove the insides and cook in boiling water for five minutes. Drain. Chop the onion and cook in corn oil until soft, add the skinned and sliced tomatoes and washed and chopped mushrooms in the last five minutes of cooking. Wash and cook the rice in boiling water. Mix the cooked rice and cheese with the onion, mushrooms, beaten egg, tomatoes, herbs and seasoning. Pile into the pepper cases and put on a greased dish with a cover.
Bake in oven set at 400 deg F (Mark 6) for 30-40 minutes.

MUSHROOM RICE

Ingredients:

3 oz brown rice	2 onions
4-6 oz mushrooms	corn oil
4-6 oz grated Cheddar cheese	2 eggs
seasoning	1 teaspoon yeast extract

Method:

Wash and cook the rice in boiling water till tender. Peel and chop the onions and fry in corn oil till golden. Wash and roughly chop the mushrooms and add to the onions in the last five minutes of cooking. Beat the eggs and mix with the grated cheese, seasoning, yeast extract, onions and mushrooms and rice. Place in a greased baking dish.

Bake in oven set at 400 deg F (Mark 6) for 30-40 minutes.

RICE STUFFING OR SAVOURY

Ingredients:

4 oz brown rice	4 oz grated Cheddar cheese
1 small red or green pepper	2 large onions
1 teaspoon sage	4 oz mushrooms
3 hard-boiled eggs	corn oil
	seasoning

Method:

Wash and cook the rice in boiling water till tender. Peel and chop the onions and cook in corn oil until golden. Add the washed and chopped pepper and the washed and roughly chopped mushrooms in the last five minutes of cooking. Mix cheese, the onions, pepper and mushrooms with the flavouring and chopped hard boiled eggs and rice. Use as required. For a savoury put in a greased baking dish and bake in oven set at 400 deg F (Mark 6) for 30 minutes.

NUT SAVOURIES

SHEPHERD'S PIE

Ingredients:

1 egg	3 oz ground cashew nuts
2 oz fresh brown breadcrumbs	1 tablespoon soya flour
1 teaspoon mixed herbs	1 teaspoon sage
2 onions	corn oil
1 large carrot	little vegetable stock
Topping	
1 lb mashed potatoes	1 egg

Method:

Peel and chop the onions and fry in corn oil till golden. Grate the carrot very fine. Crumble the breadcrumbs, beat the egg and mix all together with the herbs, ground nuts and soya flour. If too dry add vegetable stock to make moist. Place in a greased baking dish and cover with the mixture of mashed potatoes and beaten egg. Dot with margarine.

Bake in oven set at 400 deg F (Mark 6) for 40-45 minutes.

SCOTCH EGG

Ingredients:

1 dessertspoon corn oil	2 hard-boiled eggs
1 small tin Nuttolene	6 oz fresh brown breadcrumbs
seasoning	1 dessertspoon mixed herbs
	$\frac{1}{2}$ cup milk

Method:

Mix the breadcrumbs, Nuttolene, corn oil, herbs and seasoning with the milk to form a dough. Put half the mixture in a greased baking dish, place the sliced hard boiled eggs on top, and finally the remaining mixture firmly pressed down. Dot with margarine.

Bake in oven set at 400 deg F (Mark 6) for 30-40 minutes.

NUTMEAT SAVOURY

Ingredients:

½ pint brown gravy
1 small tin Nuttolene

corn oil
1 small tin sausalatas
4 medium onions

Method:

Pour enough corn oil into a baking tray to cover the bottom and put in the oven. When hot, put in the cut-up sausalatas and Nuttolene for about 30 minutes. Peel and chop the onions and cook in corn oil till golden. Add the onions to the Nuttolene and sausalatas and return to the oven for a further 30 minutes. Make up half pint of brown gravy till very thick and pour over the savoury and serve.

Bake in oven set at 400 deg F (Mark 6) for 60 minutes.

SANDY POINT STEAMED SAVOURY

Ingredients:

½ lb ground cashew nuts
4 oz fresh brown breadcrumbs
3 eggs
1 dessertspoon yeast extract

seasoning
2 onions
2 oz corn oil
½ lb skinned tomatoes
1 teaspoon herbs

Method:

Peel and chop the onions and fry in the corn oil until golden. Beat the eggs. Mix all the ingredients together with the chopped tomatoes and place in a greased pudding bowl, cover with greaseproof paper and tinfoil. Steam for two hours. Serve with tomato sauce.

This savoury can also be baked in oven set at 400 deg F (Mark 6) for 45 minutes by putting in a greased baking dish and covering with tinfoil.

SAUSALATA BATTER PUDDING

Ingredients:

4 oz wholemeal s/r flour	2 eggs
¼ pint milk	½ teaspoon salt
1 small tin sausalatas	corn oil
seasoning	

Method:

Chop the sausalatas in quarters and put in a baking dish with corn oil. Put in a moderate oven for ten minutes. Make up the batter with the flour, eggs, salt and milk and pour over the sausalatas. Return to the oven for further 30-35 minutes or until set and golden. Bake in oven set at 400 deg F (Mark 6).

NUTTOLENE BATTER PUDDING

Ingredients:

4 oz wholemeal s/r flour	¼ pint milk
2 eggs	¼ teaspoon salt
1 onion	1 small tin Nuttolene
corn oil	

Method:

Peel and chop the onion and fry in corn oil till tender. Chop the Nuttolene in quarters and put in well greased baking dish and cook in a moderate oven for ten minutes. Remove from the oven and put onions over the Nuttolene. Make up the batter with the flour, salt, eggs and milk and pour over the onion and Nuttolene. Return to the oven for a further 30-35 minutes. Bake in oven set at 400 deg F (Mark 6).

TOMATO AND NUT ROAST

Ingredients:

4 oz grated Cheddar cheese	seasoning
4 oz mixed groundnuts	8 oz tomatoes
2 oz fresh brown breadcrumbs	2 onions
1 heaped teaspoon mixed herbs	2 eggs
	corn oil

Method:

Peel and chop the onions and fry in the corn oil until tender. Skin and chop the tomatoes. Beat the eggs. Mix all the ingredients together and place in a greased baking dish.

Bake in oven set at 400 deg F (Mark 6) for 35-40 minutes.

NUT AND MUSHROOM ROAST

Ingredients:

2 onions	4 oz mushrooms
3 oz groundnuts (cashew)	2 oz fresh brown breadcrumbs
4-6 oz grated Cheddar cheese	1 teaspoon yeast extract
1 teaspoon mixed herbs	2 eggs
seasoning	corn oil

Method:

Peel and chop the onions and cook in corn oil till golden. Add the washed and roughly chopped mushrooms in the last five minutes of cooking. Mix the breadcrumbs, cheese, mixed herbs, seasoning, extract and beaten eggs with the nuts and onion and mushroom mixture. Place in a greased baking dish.

Bake in oven set at 400 deg F (Mark 6) for 35-45 minutes.

NUT AND RICE RISSOLES

Ingredients:

4 oz brown rice	golden breadcrumbs
3 oz fresh brown breadcrumbs	2 oz ground nuts
1 teaspoon curry powder	2 onions
corn oil	1 teaspoon chopped parsley
	2 eggs

Method:

Wash the rice and cook in boiling water with the peeled and chopped onions. Mix the fresh breadcrumbs with the nuts, parsley, curry powder, rice, onions and beaten egg. Cool and form into rissoles. Place on a baking tray with corn oil.

Bake in oven set at 425 deg F (Mark 7) for 30 minutes, turn at 15 minutes.

MIXED NUT RISSOLES

Ingredients:

4 oz mixed ground nuts	1 oz fresh brown breadcrumbs
2 Shredded Wheat sections	2 eggs
2 onions	$\frac{1}{2}$ cup chopped parsley
seasoning	corn oil

Method:

Peel and chop the onions and boil in water till tender. Drain. Beat the eggs, and mix with the ground nuts, crumbled breadcrumbs, Shredded Wheat sections (also crumbled), onions, seasoning and parsley. Cool. Form into rissoles and roll in golden breadcrumbs. Heat a baking tray covered with corn oil, and place the rissoles on the tray.

Bake in oven set at 425 deg F (Mark 7) for 30 minutes. Turn at 15 minutes.

CASHEW NUT RISSOLES

Ingredients:

4 oz ground cashew nuts	4 oz finely grated carrots
4 oz grated Cheddar cheese	2 eggs
seasoning	1 teaspoon chopped mint
golden breadcrumbs	1 teaspoon yeast extract
corn oil	

Method:

Mix together the ground cashew nuts, grated carrots, grated cheese, seasoning, chopped mint, yeast extract and beaten eggs. Form into rissoles and roll in the golden breadcrumbs. Heat a baking tray with corn oil, and place the rissoles on the tray.
Bake in oven set at 425 deg F (Mark 7) for 30 minutes. Turn at 15 minutes.

CASHEW NUT ROAST

Ingredients:

2 large onions	corn oil
4 oz ground cashew nuts	2 oz fresh brown breadcrumbs
4-6 oz grated Cheddar cheese	1 teaspoon yeast extract
1 teaspoon mixed herbs	2 eggs
seasoning	

Method:

Peel and chop the onions and cook in corn oil till golden. Beat the eggs. Add to the remaining ingredients, mix well and put in a greased baking dish.
Bake in oven set at 400 deg F (Mark 6) for 30-45 minutes.

CASHEW SAVOURY

Ingredients:

1 large onion
6 oz tomatoes
½ teaspoon sage
4 oz grated Cheddar cheese
seasoning

3 oz ground cashew nuts
1 oz fresh brown breadcrumbs
1 teaspoon yeast extract
corn oil
2 eggs

Method:

Peel and chop the onion and cook in corn oil until golden. Skin the tomatoes and chop. Mix together the ground nuts, breadcrumbs, extract, onions, tomatoes, sage, seasoning, grated cheese and beaten eggs. Place in a greased baking dish.
Bake in oven set at 400 deg F (Mark 6) for 40-45 minutes.

NUT SAVOURY

Ingredients:

2 large onions
4 oz fresh brown breadcrumbs
1 dessertspoon yeast extract
1 teaspoon mixed herbs
1 oz margarine

3 oz grated Cheddar cheese
4 oz ground nuts
2 eggs
1 tablespoon tomato paste
corn oil

Method:

Peel and chop the onions and cook in corn oil till golden. Mix the onions with the ground nuts, breadcrumbs, extract, herbs, tomato paste and beaten eggs and cheese. Place in a greased baking dish. Dot with margarine.
Bake in oven set at 400 deg F (Mark 6) for 30-35 minutes.

HAZELNUT PIE

Ingredients:

2 oz ground hazelnuts	2 eggs
4-6 oz grated Cheddar cheese	4 oz Shreddies or crushed
1 teaspoon mixed herbs	Shredded Wheat
seasoning	
Filling	
2 large onions	corn oil
½ medium cabbage	

Method:

Peel and chop the onions and cook in the corn oil, adding the washed and well chopped cabbage, and cook till tender. Mix the ground hazelnuts, cheese, crushed Shreddies and beaten eggs with the mixed herbs and seasoning. Place half the mixture in a greased baking dish. On top of this place the onion and cabbage mixture and top this with the remaining nut mixture. Pack down and dot with margarine.

Bake in oven set at 400 deg F (Mark 6) for 30-45 minutes or till golden.

COLD SWEETS

FRESH FRUIT SALAD

Ingredients:

¼ lb grapes	2 dessert apples
2 pears	2 bananas
1 orange	juice of 1 lemon
1 tablespoon honey	1 flat teaspoon Agar Agar
½ pint unsweetened pineapple juice	

Method:

Peel and pip the grapes, slice the pears (peeling only if necessary), grate the apples fairly fine, slice the bananas, peel and pip the orange and cut into rings and halve. Arrange all in a dish. Heat Agar Agar with the pineapple juice until dissolved, add the honey and lemon juice. Cool and pour over the fruit.

WINTER FRUIT SALAD

Ingredients:

4 oz prunes	½ pint water
4 oz dried apricots	1 banana
2 oranges	juice and rind of 1 lemon
2 tablespoons honey	4 oz dates (chopped in half)
1 teaspoon Agar Agar	

Method:

Soak the prunes and apricots in the water overnight. Next day simmer in the liquid with the Agar Agar and honey. Cool and add the sliced banana, sections of oranges and dates. Add the lemon juice and rind. Serve with cream.

MUESLI

Ingredients for individual portions:

3 tablespoons water or milk
1 tablespoon oats
1 teaspoon honey or black
    treacle
grated rind of orange or
    lemon

1 eating apple
1 tablespoon raisins
1 dessertspoon ground nuts
top of milk or cream

Method:

Soak the oats and raisins in the water or milk overnight.
In the morning add the grated apples (unpeeled), the
honey and ground nuts and mix thoroughly. Sprinkle
with some grated orange rind and pour over some top
of milk or cream.

QUICK MUESLI

Ingredients:

1 dessert apple per person
1 dessertspoon raisins per
    person

2 tablespoons rolled oats per
    person
milk

Method:

Grate the apple very fine and add the oats and raisins.
When ready to serve pour over hot or cold milk as
required. Sugar or honey can be added if needed, also
lemon juice and ground nuts if required.

GOOSEBERRY FOOL

Ingredients:

1 lb gooseberries	brown sugar or honey to taste
¼ pint water	½ pint egg custard or cream

Method:

Top and tail the gooseberries and wash. Simmer in the water till cooked. Rub through a sieve or liquidize. Add the honey; when quite cold add the egg custard or cream and whip.

BLACKBERRY FOOL

Ingredients:

1 lb blackberries	water to stew fruit
1 teaspoon Agar Agar	1 tablespoon honey
½ pint egg custard or cream	

Method:

Heat the water in a saucepan and add the Agar Agar. Bring to the boil, add the washed fruit and simmer slowly. Sieve or liquidize and cool. Add the honey. When cooled add the egg custard or cream and whip well.

APPLE SNOW

Ingredients:

2 cooking apples	honey to taste
2 egg whites	2 egg yolks

Method:

Cook the peeled apples to a pulp and add the honey, cool and add egg yolks. Whisk the egg whites and fold into the cooled apples. Chill and serve with grated chocolate.

APRICOT SNOW

Ingredients:

½ lb dried or fresh apricots   2 egg yolks
rind of 1 lemon   2 egg whites
    1 teaspoon honey

Method:

If dried soak the apricots overnight; in the morning, liquidize fruit with a little water to make a purée and add the lemon rind, egg yolks and honey. Whisk the egg whites until stiff and fold into the purée and chill before serving.

BLACKCURRANT JELLY

Ingredients:

¾ pint water   2 teaspoons Agar Agar
¼ pint blackcurrant juice

Method:

Bring the water to boil with the Agar Agar and add the blackcurrant juice to taste and pour into a mould to set. This can be done with any flavour, orange, lemon juice, etc., and fruit can also be added before pouring into a mould to set.

BANANA WHIP

Ingredients:

4 ripe bananas   grated lemon rind
½ pint of vegetarian lemon
  jelly

Method:

Peel and mash the bananas with the grated lemon rind. Make up the jelly and when beginning to set whisk the bananas in. Chill and serve.

ORANGE FLUFF

Ingredients:

2 medium oranges	2 eggs
1 tablespoon honey	small tin mandarines

Method:

Wash the oranges and grate the rinds. Squeeze the juice. Mix the rind and juice with the honey and egg yolks. Put in a basin over hot water and cook, stirring, till thick. Remove from the heat and cool. Whisk the egg whites till stiff and fold in, with the mandarines, to the cooled mixture.

ALMOND FLUFF

Ingredients:

½ pint milk	1 egg
3 oz ground almonds	1 tablespoon honey
1 teaspoon Agar Agar	1 teaspoon almond essence

Method:

Well heat the milk and Agar Agar, stir and cook for a few minutes. Add the almond essence, ground almonds and sugar with the egg yolk. Cool the mixture. Beat the egg white till stiff and fold into the almond mixture. Cool and serve, sprinkled with halved almonds.

JUNKET

Ingredients:

1 pint milk	2 teaspoons Agar Agar
2 tablespoons honey	½ teaspoon vanilla essence

Method:

Bring the milk nearly to the boil with the Agar Agar for a few minutes. Add the honey and stir till melted. Add the essence and put in a mould to set.

APPLE FOAM

Ingredients:

½ lb cooking apples   4 oz brown sugar or honey
1 lemon   ¼ pint milk
1 teaspoon Agar Agar   2 eggs

Method:

Peel and cut the apples and cook in a little water till pulpy. Stir in the sugar and grated lemon rind and egg yolks. Heat the milk with the Agar Agar for a few minutes, stirring. Stir the milk into the apple pulp and whisk. Whisk the egg whites and fold into the apple mixture and cool thoroughly.

VANILLA ICE CREAM

Ingredients:

½ pint milk   3 oz honey or sugar
3 egg yolks   ½ pint evaporated milk
vanilla essence

Method:

Warm the milk with the sugar or honey, add a few drops of vanilla essence and pour on to egg yolks, beating all the time. Heat till thick, then cool. Whip the evaporated milk until stiff, fold into the mixture and turn into a freezing tray. Freeze. When half-frozen put into a bowl and whisk thoroughly. Return to freezing tray and freeze until firm. For chocolate ice cream grate 2 oz chocolate, melt and add to the custard instead of the honey.

WATER ICE

Ingredients:

½ pint fruit juice	1 tablespoon lemon juice
honey to taste	2 egg whites

Method:

Warm and sweeten the fruit juice with honey till dissolved. Add the lemon juice and when cold put in freezer. Stir in 15 minutes. Turn into a chilled mixing bowl and fold in the whisked egg whites: replace in the refrigerator and freeze. Serve with fruit, preferably the same as the juice.

EGG CUSTARD

Ingredients:

½ pint milk	1 egg
1 teaspoon Agar Agar	1 dessertspoon honey or
few drops vanilla essence	brown sugar

Method:

Gently heat the milk with the Agar Agar for a few minutes until very hot. Add the beaten egg and honey and cook slowly for further time, stirring. Add the essence and cook till thickened. This can be liquidized or whisked until smooth and creamy. The custard can be baked in the oven if desired.

COFFEE SAUCE

Ingredients:

| 1 teacup black coffee | 1 teacup milk |
| 2 egg yolks | 1 dessertspoon honey |

Method:

Mix the egg yolks. Heat the coffee and milk with the honey and pour slowly on to the yolks, stirring until the sauce thickens, but do not bring to boil. Serve with any hot pudding.

HOT SWEETS

STUFFED BAKED APPLES

Ingredients:

2 lb even-sized cooking apples	6 oz chopped dates
½ oz margarine	3 oz brown sugar
½ teaspoon ground cinnamon	little water

Method:

Wipe and core the apples, cut each across with a sharp knife at the top and scoop out a little apple. Fill the cavity with the chopped dates, sugar, cinnamon and scooped-out apple mixed well together. Place on a greased baking tray or shallow heat-proof dish and surround with a little water. Cover the apples with grease-proof paper.

Bake in oven set at 350 deg F (Mark 4) for 45 minutes.

APPLE SOUFFLE

Ingredients:

3 large cooking apples	2 eggs
2 oz brown sugar	½ teaspoon ground cloves
grated rind of ½ lemon	

Method:

Peel and core the apples and cook in a little water till pulpy. Beat the sugar and egg yolks with the lemon rind and ground cloves, add the apple and mix. Whisk the egg whites until stiff and fold into the mixture. Pour into a greased baking dish.

Bake in oven set at 400 deg F (Mark 6) for 20-30 minutes.

APPLE PANCAKES

Ingredients:

2 cooking apples
2 tablespoons brown sugar
juice ½ lemon
grated rind of lemon

2 eggs
2 tablespoons wholemeal s/r
 flour
pinch cinnamon
corn oil

Method:

Cream the sugar and egg yolks. Peel and grate the apples and add to the sugar and yolks, mix in the flour, ground cinnamon and lemon juice and rind. Whisk the egg whites and fold in. Heat a little corn oil in pan and cook small pancakes, turn when underside cooked. Sprinkle with a little brown sugar before serving.

APPLE BATTER

Ingredients:

1 lb cooking apples
2 tablespoons brandy or
 lemon juice

brown sugar to taste

Batter
4 oz wholemeal s/r flour
pinch nutmeg
½ pint milk

2 eggs
3 oz brown sugar

Method:

Peel and slice the apples and mix with the sugar and brandy and put in a greased casserole. Gradually combine the batter ingredients together and when smooth pour over the apples.
Bake in oven set at 400 deg F (Mark 6) for 45 minutes.

ALMOND AND APPLE PUDDING

Ingredients:

1 lb cooking apples	1 oz raisins
1 tablespoon lemon juice	3 oz brown sugar
Topping	
4 oz margarine	2 oz ground almonds
4 oz brown sugar	2 oz wholemeal flour
2 eggs	almond essence

Method:

Peel and slice the apples and cook with the sugar, raisins and lemon juice in a little water till tender. Grease a pudding dish and place in it the cooked apple mixture. Cream the margarine and sugar, beat the eggs and add slowly. Fold in the almonds and flour with a few drops of almond essence. Place this mixture on the apples.

Bake in oven set at 400 deg F (Mark 6) for 30-35 minutes.

ALMOND AND FRUIT PUDDING

Ingredients:

1 lb cooking apples	½ pint milk
2 eggs	6 oz brown sugar
4 oz ground almonds	pinch nutmeg

Method:

Peel and grate the apples, mix with the almonds and put in a greased dish. Heat the milk and add the sugar, beat in the eggs and nutmeg and pour over the apple mixture.

Bake at 400 deg F (Mark 6) for 45 minutes until set.

APRICOT AND GINGER CRUMBLE

Ingredients:

12 oz apricots	3 oz ground almonds
3 oz margarine	almond essence
4 oz wholemeal s/r flour	½ teaspoon ground ginger
	3 oz brown sugar

Method:

Put the apricots into an ovenproof dish and sprinkle with almond essence. Rub the margarine into the flour and ginger until mixed. Add the sugar and ground almonds with the flour mixture. Sprinkle over the apricots.

Bake in oven set at 375 deg F (Mark 5) for 35-40 minutes.

PLUM OR DAMSON CRUMBLE

Ingredients:

1 lb plums	3 oz margarine
3 tablespoons water	6 oz brown sugar
1 teaspoon ground cinnamon	2 oz wholemeal s/r flour
	4 oz oats

Method:

Wash the plums or damsons well and cut in half removing the stones. Place the fruit in a greased pie dish, sprinkle with half the sugar and pour the water over. Mix the flour and cinnamon together, add the oats and rub in the margarine. Stir in the remaining sugar and sprinkle the mixture over the fruit.

Bake in oven set at 350 deg F (Mark 4) for 45 minutes.

APRICOT AND APPLE FLAN

Ingredients:

6 oz shortcrust pastry
6 oz wholemeal s/r flour   3 oz margarine
water to mix

Filling
1 lb small cooking apples   1 tablespoon brown sugar
3 tablespoons sieved apricot
jam

Method:

Roll out the pastry and line an eight inch flan tin. Peel the apples and cut into very thin slices. Arrange in the flan in a circle, overlapping: fill well as apples shrink when cooking. Sprinkle with the sugar. Cover with the sieved hot apricot jam when removed from oven.
Bake in oven set at 400 deg F (Mark 6) for 25 minutes.
Reduce to 355 deg F (Mark 4) for 15 minutes.

CINNAMON APPLE CRISP

Ingredients:

1½ lb cooking apples   6 oz wholemeal s/r flour
8 oz brown sugar   2 eggs
4 oz melted margarine   1 teaspoon ground cinnamon

Method:

Peel and core and slice the apples into an ovenproof dish, in layers, with half the sugar. Mix the flour and remaining sugar and add the eggs and ground cinnamon together. Spread on top of the apples and pour over the melted margarine.
Bake in oven set at 350 deg F (Mark 4) for 30 minutes.

FRUIT CRISP

Ingredients:

1 lb apples or plums	4 oz wholemeal s/r flour
4-6 oz brown sugar	½ teaspoon ground cloves
2 oz margarine	little water

Method:

Slice the fruit and lay in a pie dish with a little water and 3-4 oz sugar. Rub the margarine into the flour, add the remaining sugar and ground cloves and mix well. Sprinkle thickly over the surface of the fruit.

Bake in oven set at 400 deg F (Mark 6) until the crust is golden and the fruit tender.

APRICOT AMBER

Ingredients:

4 oz shortcrust pastry

4 oz wholemeal s/r flour	2 oz margarine
water to mix	1 oz brown sugar

Filling

1½ lb apricots or apples	2 eggs
3 oz brown sugar	2 oz melted margarine

Method:

Line the pie dish with pastry. Sieve or liquidize the apricots and mix with the sugar, add the egg yolks and melted margarine. Pour into the pie dish. Whisk the egg whites until stiff and add a little sugar. Bake without the meringue at first.

Bake in oven set at 400 deg F (Mark 6) for 30 minutes. Remove from oven, pile on the egg whites and return to oven till the top is crisp.

CUSTARD TART

Ingredients:

4 oz shortcrust pastry
4 oz wholemeal s/r flour   1 oz brown sugar
2½ oz margarine   water to mix

Filling
½ pint milk   ½ teaspoon vanilla essence
1 egg   ½ teaspoon ground nutmeg
1 tablespoon honey   1 teaspoon Agar Agar

Method:

Make up the pastry and line a pie dish. Beat the egg. Put the milk and honey in a saucepan and heat well, with the Agar Agar and vanilla essence, for a few minutes. Add the beaten egg and stir. Cool and pour into the pastry case.

Bake at 400 deg F (Mark 6) till the pastry is set, lower the temperature and let the custard set.

BLACKBERRY TART

Ingredients:

8 oz shortcrust pastry
8 oz wholemeal s/r flour   2 oz brown sugar
4 oz margarine   water to mix

Filling
1 lb blackberries   juice and rind of 1 lemon
top of milk   brown sugar to taste

Method:

Roll out the pastry and line a fireproof pie plate. Roll out left-over pastry into strips for top. Mix the fruit with the lemon juice and rind and sugar to taste. Fill the pie and put the pastry strips, trellised, over the top. Brush with top of milk.

Bake in oven set at 450 deg F (Mark 8) for about 30 minutes.

DATE AND APPLE PASTIES

Ingredients:

    8 oz shortcrust pastry

    8 oz wholemeal s/r flour   4 oz margarine

    water to mix   1 oz brown sugar

    Filling

    1 lb cooking apples   4 oz dates

    2 oz brown sugar   1 beaten egg to glaze

Method:

Roll out the pastry and cut into rounds about four inches wide. Peel and chop the apples. Chop the dates. Mix the apples, dates and sugar together and place mixture in the middle of each round of pastry. Brush the edges with water and pinch together to form pasties. Remove thick corners and press. Brush with beaten egg. Place on baking sheet.
Bake in oven set at 400 deg F (Mark 6) for 20-30 minutes.

FRUIT PIE

Ingredients:

    Topping

    6 oz wholemeal s/r flour   4 oz well-chopped nuts

    3 oz margarine   water to bind

    Fruit

    2 lb cooking apples   4 oz stoned dates

    1 teaspoon mixed spice   2 oz brown sugar

Method:

Peel, core and slice the apples, put into the pie dish with the chopped dates and sprinkle with the spice and sugar. Mix the flour and margarine with water to make a pastry dough and add the nuts. Roll this out and cover the fruit.
Bake at 400 deg F (Mark 6) for 30 minutes.

PLATE APPLE PIE

Ingredients:

8 *oz shortcrust pastry*
8 oz wholemeal s/r flour   4 oz margarine
water to mix

Filling
1 lb cooking apples   2 oz raisins
4 oz brown sugar   ¼ teaspoon ground cinnamon
    egg white for glaze

Method:

Roll out the pastry and line the plate. Trim the edges. Peel, core and slice the apples and place them in layers with the raisins. Mix the cinnamon and sugar and sprinkle over the apples. Roll out the remaining pastry and, after moistening the top of the pastry rim, place on top and press edges together and pinch. Brush with egg white.
Bake in oven set at 400 deg F (Mark 6) for 35-40 minutes.

APPLE PIE

Ingredients:

8 *oz shortcrust pastry*
8 oz wholemeal s/r flour   4 oz margarine
water to mix

Filling
2 lb cooking apples   6 oz brown sugar
3 cloves   1 beaten egg to glaze
lemon juice   3 tablespoons water

Method:

Make the pastry. Peel and core the apples and cut in slices. Put in pie dish in layers with the sugar between.

Put the cloves between the apples and add three table-spoons water with a little lemon juice over the apples. Roll out a strip of pastry to fit the rim. Roll the remaining pastry. Brush edges with water and cover pie. Flute edges and brush top with beaten egg. Bake in oven set at 400 deg F (Mark 6) for 15 minutes. Reduce to 355 deg F (Mark 4) for further 20-25 minutes until cooked.

APPLE AND OAT PIE

Ingredients:
  6 *oz shortcrust pastry*

6 oz wholemeal s/r flour	3 oz margarine
water to mix	1 oz brown sugar

  Filling

2 lb cooking apples	1 teaspoon ground cinnamon
4 oz brown sugar	

  Topping

3 oz margarine	3 oz brown sugar
2 tablespoons black treacle	6 oz oats

Method:

Roll out the pastry and line a pie dish. Peel, core and slice the apples and layer with the sugar mixed with the cinnamon into the dish. Melt the margarine, sugar and treacle in a pan, stir in the oats and spread over the top of the apples.

Bake in oven set at 400 deg F (Mark 6) for 10-15 minutes, reducing to 350 deg F (Mark 4) for 20-30 minutes.

INDIVIDUAL APPLE PIES

Ingredients:

8 oz shortcrust pastry
8 oz wholemeal s/r flour   4 oz margarine
water to mix

Filling
1 lb cooking apples   beaten egg for glaze
3 oz brown sugar

Method:

Line deep tartlet tins with the thinly rolled out pastry. Peel and core the apples and chop quite small, mix with the sugar and fill the tartlets to the top. Moisten the edges, put on the rolled out pastry tops and pinch together, trim and flute. Brush with beaten egg.
Bake in oven set at 400 deg F (Mark 6) for 20-25 minutes. Remove pies from tins and put on a baking sheet.

GINGER PUDDING

Ingredients:

4 oz wholemeal s/r flour   2 eggs
2 teaspoons ground ginger   1 tablespoon milk
3 oz margarine   3 oz brown sugar

Method:

Mix the flour and ginger, add the margarine, sugar and eggs with the milk and beat well together until mixed. Place in a well greased pudding basin, cover with greaseproof paper and baking foil and steam for $1\frac{1}{2}$ to 2 hours.

ALMOND CHOCOLATE PIE

Ingredients:

6 oz orange shortcrust pastry

6 oz wholemeal s/r flour	1 tablespoon grated orange
1 oz brown sugar	rind
1 tablespoon orange juice	3 oz margarine

Filling

4 oz margarine	milk to mix
2 eggs	4 oz brown sugar
4 oz wholemeal s/r flour	3 oz flaked almonds
	½ oz cocoa

Method:

Roll out the pastry to line a pie dish. Mix the margarine and sugar and add the eggs, beat well, add the almonds, flour and cocoa and mix in. Add enough milk to give soft dropping consistency and put into pastry and spread evenly.

Bake in oven set at 400 deg F (Mark 6) for 45-50 minutes.

SPONGE PUDDING

Ingredients:

3 oz margarine	pinch mixed spice
2 eggs	3 oz brown sugar
2 tablespoons jam	4 oz wholemeal s/r flour
	milk to mix

Method:

Grease a basin and put the jam at the bottom. Cream the margarine and sugar and add to the eggs and half the flour. Add the milk with the remaining flour and mix to dropping consistency with the spice added. Put in the basin and cover with greaseproof paper and baking foil. Steam until well-risen and firm for 1½ to 2 hours.

CHOCOLATE PUDDING (BAKED)

Ingredients:

6 oz wholemeal s/r flour	$\frac{1}{2}$ teaspoon powdered nutmeg
2 oz cocoa	4 oz margarine
4 oz brown sugar	2 eggs
milk to mix	few drops vanilla essence

Method:

Mix the margarine with the flour and add the sugar and the rest of the dry ingredients. Beat the eggs and add with enough milk to make a soft dough. Turn into a greased baking dish.
Bake in oven set at 400 deg F (Mark 6) for 35-45 minutes.

CHOCOLATE PUDDING (STEAMED)

Ingredients:

3 oz plain block chocolate	2 tablespoons milk
3 oz margarine	3 oz brown sugar
1 egg	vanilla essence
$\frac{1}{2}$ oz cocoa powder	4 oz wholemeal s/r flour

Method:

Grease a one-and-a-half pint pudding basin. Break the chocolate into small pieces and place with the milk in a saucepan; heat gently until the chocolate is melted and smooth. Cool. Cream the margarine and sugar with a few drops of vanilla essence. Slowly beat in the melted chocolate. Beat in the egg a little at a time and fold in the flour and cocoa. Turn the mixture into the basin, cover with greaseproof paper and baking foil and cook in steamer for $1\frac{1}{2}$ to 2 hours.

EVE'S PUDDING

Ingredients:

1 lb cooking apples	½ teaspoon ground cloves
4 oz brown sugar	1 teaspoon water
1 egg	2 oz margarine
	2 oz wholemeal s/r flour

Method:

Peel and slice the apples and put them into a pie dish with 2 oz sugar and the water. Cream the margarine and remaining sugar and beat in the egg. Stir in the flour and ground cloves and put the mixture on top of the fruit.

Bake in oven set at 400 deg F (Mark 6) for 40-60 minutes till well risen and golden.

PINEAPPLE PUDDING

Ingredients:

1 medium can pineapple rings	1 oz margarine
1 oz brown sugar	4 oz margarine
4 oz brown sugar	grated rind and juice of lemon
4 oz wholemeal s/r flour	2 eggs

Method:

Melt the 1 oz margarine and pour into bottom of seven to eight inch cake tin. Sprinkle with the 1 oz sugar and 1 tablespoon pineapple juice. Put on the pineapple rings. Cream the margarine and sugar and stir in the lemon rind, beat in the eggs and lemon juice with the flour. Spread the mixture over the fruit.

Bake in oven set at 400 deg F (Mark 6) for 45 minutes.

BAKED ORANGE PUDDING

Ingredients:

4 oz wholemeal s/r flour	4 oz margarine
4 oz brown sugar	2 eggs
grated rind of 1 orange	about 2 tablespoons orange
1 teaspoon ground cinnamon	juice
1 tin mandarins	2 oz brown sugar

Method:

Grease a dish and sprinkle with the 2 oz brown sugar. Cream the margarine and 4 oz sugar and gradually add the eggs. Stir in the flour, cinnamon and orange rind with enough juice to make a soft consistency. Put into the prepared dish and bake.
Bake in oven set at 400 deg F (Mark 6) for 45 minutes.
Serve with mardarins.

NUTMEG AND ORANGE PUDDING

Ingredients:

1 grated orange rind	4 oz wholemeal s/r flour
4 oz margarine	4 oz brown sugar
2 eggs	milk to mix
grated nutmeg	

Method:

Rub the margarine into the flour and add the sugar. Beat in the eggs. Add milk and orange rind and pour into greased baking dish. Sprinkle with nutmeg.
Bake in oven set at 400 deg F (Mark 6) for 45 minutes.

MERINGUE SPICED PUDDING

Ingredients:

6 oz margarine
6 oz brown sugar
2 egg yolks
6 oz wholemeal s/r flour
   Topping
2 egg whites
4 oz light brown sugar

1 teaspoon ground ginger
2 oz stem ginger
1 egg
1 teaspoon mixed spice

3 oz nuts (well chopped)

Method:

Grease and line a seven inch square cake tin. Cream the margarine and sugar together and beat in the egg yolks and the egg. Fold in the flour, ground ginger and mixed spice. Chop the stem ginger and add to the mixture. Place in the prepared tin. Beat the egg whites until stiff, fold gently in the sugar and nuts, and pile on the pudding.

Bake in oven set at 350 deg F (Mark 5) for 45-60 minutes.

CAKES, BISCUITS AND BREADS

ALMOND AND CHOCOLATE CAKE

Ingredients:

4 oz margarine	1 dessertspoon orange juice
4 oz ground almonds	4 oz brown sugar
2 large eggs	2 oz wholemeal s/r flour
few drops almond essence	2 oz plain chocolate
grated rind of orange	pinch cinnamon
	$\frac{1}{4}$ teaspoon ground cloves

Method:

Cream the margarine and sugar with the almond essence, grated rind of orange and spices. Add the softened chocolate and almonds and mix well. Add the flour and beaten eggs together with the orange juice. Turn into a greased and lined loaf tin. When cooked and cooled coat with the following.

4 oz chocolate	nob of margarine
1 teaspoon orange juice	

Melt the margarine and chocolate and orange juice and immediately coat the cake.

Bake in oven set at 400 deg F (Mark 6) for 45-55 minutes.

CHERRY CAKE

Ingredients:

8 oz wholemeal s/r flour	1 grated rind of lemon
6 oz brown sugar	6 oz margarine
8 oz glacé cherries	3 eggs
	1 tablespoon lemon juice

Method:

Cream the margarine and sugar and add the beaten eggs. Fold in the flour and lemon rind, add the lemon juice and, finally, fold in the halved and floured glacé cherries. Put in a greased and lined loaf tin.

Bake in oven set at 400 deg F (Mark 6) for 50-60 minutes.

CHOCOLATE ORANGE CAKE

Ingredients:

6 oz margarine	6 oz brown sugar
3 eggs	6 oz wholemeal s/r flour
2 grated orange rinds	juice of orange to mix

Method:

Cream well together the margarine and sugar. Mix in the beaten eggs and add the flour and orange rinds. Add some juice of the oranges to form a soft dropping consistency. Put into a greased and lined loaf tin.

When cooked coat with 4 oz melted chocolate with a few drops of vanilla essence and a little margarine stirred well together.

Bake in oven set at 400 deg F (Mark 6) for 50-60 minutes.

CHOCOLATE CAKE

Ingredients:

6 oz wholemeal s/r flour	6 oz margarine
6 oz brown sugar	4 level tablespoons cocoa
3 eggs	¼ teaspoon vanilla essence
2 oz ground almonds	milk to mix

Method:

Mix the flour and sugar together with the almonds and add the margarine. Mix the cocoa in a little hot water and add with the eggs and essence. Mix well. Add the milk and mix to a soft dropping consistency. Place in greased and lined cake tin.

Bake in oven set at 400 deg F (Mark 6) for 25-30 minutes.

CHRISTMAS CAKE

Ingredients:

4 oz glacé cherries	4 oz almonds
1 orange	1 teaspoon cinnamon
6 oz raisins	1 teaspoon ground nutmeg
½ teaspoon mixed spice	5 oz currants
4 oz margarine	4 oz brown sugar
3 eggs	5 oz wholemeal s/r flour

Method:

Cream the margarine and sugar and add the eggs one at a time. Fold in the flour. Mix in the spices with the grated rind of the orange. Add the blanched almonds, well chopped, and the washed fruit well dusted with flour. Add the cherries, also dusted with flour. Turn into a round seven inch cake tin. Cook. When cooked and cold sprinkle the base and sides with brandy, about 2 tablespoonsful. Wrap in foil and store. Each week before use add more brandy as above. This should be made six to eight weeks in advance.

Bake at 275 deg F (Mark 1) for one hour, reduce to 250 deg F (Mark ½) for 3½-4 hours.

COCONUT CAKE

Ingredients:

6 oz margarine	6 oz brown sugar
3 eggs	6 oz wholemeal s/r flour
4 oz desiccated coconut	1 grated lemon rind and juice

Method:

Cream the margarine and sugar and add the beaten eggs. Fold in the flour and coconut and lemon rind. Mix well. Add lemon juice to mix. Put in a well greased and lined cake tin.

Bake in oven set at 400 deg F (Mark 6) for 35-40 minutes.

COFFEE WALNUT CAKE

Ingredients:

4 oz margarine	4 oz brown sugar
2 eggs	3 oz chopped walnuts
4 oz wholemeal s/r flour	1 tablespoon coffee powder
¼ teaspoon vanilla essence	

Method:

Cream the margarine and sugar and add the beaten eggs. Mix in the flour and coffee powder. Add the chopped walnuts and essence, mix well together and place in a greased loaf tin.
Bake in oven set at 400 deg F (Mark 6) for 35-40 minutes.

DATE CAKE

Ingredients:

8 oz wholemeal s/r flour	6 oz chopped dates
½ teaspoon mixed spice	3 oz brown sugar
3 eggs	milk to mix
4 oz margarine	

Method:

Mix together the flour and spices and rub in the margarine. Add the sugar and chopped dates. Add the beaten eggs and sufficient milk to form a dropping consistency. Put in a greased six to seven inch tin and bake.
Bake in oven set at 400 deg F (Mark 6) for 50 minutes to one hour or until firm.

99

FRUIT CAKE

Ingredients:

6 oz margarine	6 oz brown sugar
3 eggs	8 oz wholemeal s/r flour
1 tablespoon cocoa	4 oz chopped almonds
1 teaspoon nutmeg	10 oz raisins
¼ teaspoon ground cloves	1 grated orange rind

Method:

Cream the margarine and sugar and add the beaten eggs and mix in the flour and mix well. Add the spices and cocoa, mix, add the orange rind, raisins and nuts, mix well together. Place in a greased and lined baking tin.

Bake in oven set at 325 deg F (Mark 3) for $1\frac{1}{4}$-$1\frac{1}{2}$ hours.

NUT AND ORANGE CAKE

Ingredients:

8 oz wholemeal s/r flour	6 oz margarine
4 oz brown sugar	3 large eggs
1 teaspoon mixed spice	1 grated orange rind
2 oz finely chopped nuts	orange juice to mix

Method:

Cream the margarine and sugar and add the eggs one at a time. Beat well after each addition. Mix in the flour with the spice, stir in the orange rind and nuts and mix to dropipng consistency with orange juice if needed. Turn into a greased seven inch round cake tin.

Bake in oven set at 350 deg F (Mark 4) for 1-$1\frac{1}{2}$ hours.

MADEIRA CAKE

Ingredients:

6 oz margarine	6 oz brown sugar
3 eggs	8 oz wholemeal s/r flour
few drops vanilla essence	1 grated lemon rind
1 dessertspoon milk	

Method:

Cream the margarine and sugar and add the beaten eggs one at a time with the flour. Mix in the essence and lemon rind. Mix in the milk. Put in a greased and lined cake tin.
Bake in oven set at 400 deg F (Mark 6) for 45-60 minutes.

WALNUT CAKE

Ingredients:

Cake

6 oz margarine	6 oz brown sugar
½ teaspoon vanilla essence	3 large eggs
6 oz wholemeal s/r flour	4 oz chopped walnuts

Spread

4 oz margarine	4 oz brown sugar
1-2 tablespoons coffee powder	¼ teaspoon vanilla essence

Method:

Cream the margarine and sugar and add the beaten eggs and essence. Fold in the flour and when well blended add the chopped nuts. Place in a greased and lined cake tin. Cook and cool. Mix the ingredients for the spread well together and fill the cake.
Bake cake at 400 deg F (Mark 6) for 50-60 minutes.

COCONUT BUNS

Ingredients:

4 oz brown sugar	4 oz margarine
4 oz wholemeal s/r flour	milk to mix
4 oz desiccated coconut	½ teaspoon vanilla essence
2 eggs	

Method:

Cream the sugar and margarine. Add the eggs and flour. Mix in the coconut, essence and milk to give a dropping consistency. Fill bun cases two-thirds.
Bake in oven set at 400 deg F (Mark 6) for 15-20 minutes.

BATH BUNS

Ingredients:

1 lb wholemeal plain flour	pinch salt
2 oz margarine	4 oz brown sugar
1 oz fresh yeast or 2 level	8 tablespoons warm milk
dessertspoons dried yeast	8 tablespoons warm water
4 teaspoons cold milk	½ lb raisins
2 eggs	2 oz chopped mixed peel
grated rind of 1 lemon	

Method:

Sift the flour and salt into a warm bowl. Rub in margarine and 3 oz of sugar. Cream the fresh yeast with 1 teaspoon sugar, stir in the tepid milk and water. Beat the eggs, add to flour mixture and mix to soft dough. For dried yeast, sprinkle on to mixed tepid liquids with 1 teaspoon sugar and leave for 15 minutes until thick and frothy. Add to the flour with eggs and mix to a dough. Put the dough into a warm bowl and cover with

clean warm tea towel. Leave in warm place for one to one-and-a-half hours till doubled. Turn on to a floured board and knead in the raisins, lemon rind and peel. With floured hands form dough into 16 buns and place on a greased baking sheet. Leave in warm place for 20 minutes. Brush buns with cold milk and sprinkle with demerara sugar.
Bake in oven set at 400 deg F (Mark 6) for 20-25 minutes.

VANILLA BUNS

Ingredients:

6 oz wholemeal s/r flour	2 eggs
6 oz margarine	6 oz brown sugar
	1 tablespoon vanilla essence

Method:

Mix the margarine and sugar. Add the flour and mix well. Beat in the eggs and essence to dropping consistency. Put in bun cases, about two-thirds full.
Bake in oven set at 400 deg F (Mark 6) for 15-25 minutes.

HONEY BUNS

Ingredients:

1 lemon rind	milk to mix
3 oz honey	4 oz margarine
6 oz wholemeal s/r flour	2 oz chopped dates
	2 eggs

Method:

Cream the margarine and honey and add the eggs. Mix in the flour and dates and add milk for dropping consistency. Fill two-thirds of each bun case.
Bake in oven set at 400 deg F (Mark 6) for 15-20 minutes.

SPICY ORANGE BUNS

Ingredients:

5 oz wholemeal s/r flour	4 oz margarine
4 oz brown sugar	2 eggs
1 teaspoon mixed spice	1 grated orange rind
about 1 tablespoon orange juice	

Method:

Mix the dry ingredients together and add the margarine, beaten eggs and juice to give a dropping consistency. Two-thirds fill the bun cases.
Bake in oven set at 400 deg F (Mark 6) for 15-25 minutes.

FEATHER BUNS

Ingredients:

5 oz wholemeal s/r flour	4 oz margarine
4 oz brown sugar	2 eggs
about 1 tablespoon cream	

Method:

Cream together the margarine and sugar. Add the eggs and mix in the flour and cream to make a dropping consistency. Place in bun cases, filling each by two-thirds.
Bake in oven set at 400 deg F (Mark 6) for 12-15 minutes.

CHOCOLATE BUNS

Ingredients:

5 oz wholemeal s/r flour	milk to mix
4 oz margarine	2 oz cocoa
2 eggs	4 oz brown sugar
	3-4 drops vanilla essence

Method:

Cream the margarine and sugar and add the eggs, mix well. Add the flour, essence and cocoa, and milk if needed, to form a firm dropping consistency. Fill two-thirds of each bun case.
Bake in oven set at 400 deg F (Mark 6) for 15-20 minutes.

SWISS ROLL

Ingredients:

2 oz wholemeal s/r flour	jam
2 eggs	2 oz brown sugar
	1 tablespoon warm water

Method:

Line a swiss roll tin and grease. Whisk the eggs and sugar until thick and creamy, fold in half the flour and then add the warm water and stir in the remaining flour: stir until smooth. Pour into the prepared tin. When cooked place on greaseproof paper over a damp cloth and spread with warm jam, roll carefully and leave to cool on a rack. For chocolate version add four level teaspoons cocoa.
Bake in oven set at 400 deg F (Mark 6) till firm.

CUP CAKES

Ingredients:

3 oz margarine	5 oz wholemeal s/r flour
3 oz brown sugar	2 eggs
few drops vanilla essence	milk to mix

Method:

Cream the margarine and sugar. Add the beaten eggs slowly, add the vanilla essence, fold in the flour and finally mix in the milk to give a soft dropping consistency. Place in bun cases. For chocolate cakes replace one tablespoon flour by one tablespoon cocoa.
Bake in oven set at 350 deg F (Mark 3-4) for 15-20 minutes.

DATE AND LEMON CAKES

Ingredients:

8 oz wholemeal s/r flour	6 oz margarine
6 oz brown sugar	2 eggs
4 oz chopped dates	1 lemon rind
juice of lemon to mix	

Method:

Cream the margarine and sugar and add the beaten eggs and flour. Mix in the lemon rind and dates and, finally, lemon juice to form a stiff consistency. Place the mixture in bun cases.
Bake in oven set at 400 deg F (Mark 6) for 15-20 minutes.

CHOCOLATE CHIP CAKES

Ingredients:

4 oz brown sugar	4 oz margarine
2 eggs	5 oz wholemeal s/r flour
1 packet chocolate chips	few drops vanilla essence

Method:

Cream the margarine and add the sugar till mixed. Add the eggs one at a time and beat well. Fold in the flour, mix and add the essence and chocolate chips. Put in bun cases.
Bake in oven set at 350 deg F (Mark 5) for 15-20 minutes.

GINGER CAKES

Ingredients:

5 oz wholemeal s/r flour	4 oz margarine
4 oz brown sugar	2 eggs
2 teaspoons ground ginger	4 oz chopped crystallized ginger

Method:

Cream the margarine and flour and gradually add the lightly beaten eggs. Add the flour and ground ginger till blended and add the crystallized ginger. Place the mixture into bun cases.
Bake in oven set at 400 deg F (Mark 6) for 15-20 minutes.

QUEEN CAKES

Ingredients:

5 oz wholemeal s/r flour	4 oz brown sugar
4 oz margarine	6 oz raisins
2 eggs	1 grated lemon rind

Method:

Mix the sugar and margarine. Add the eggs and cream well together. Mix in the flour and grated rind and raisins. Fill the bun cases two-thirds.
Bake in oven set at 400 deg F (Mark 6) for 15-20 minutes.

APRICOT BARS

Ingredients:

4 oz dried apricots	6 oz brown sugar
3 oz margarine	2 eggs
6 oz wholemeal s/r flour	½ teaspoon vanilla essence
grated rind of 1 lemon	2 oz chopped nuts or raisins

Method:

Boil the apricots for ten minutes, drain, cool and chop. Rub the margarine into 5 oz flour and 2 oz sugar. Pack into a greased flat tin and bake for 25 minutes. Meanwhile mix the chopped apricots with 1 oz flour, vanilla essence, lemon rind, 4 oz sugar, chopped nuts and beaten eggs. When 25 minutes' cooking time is up remove from oven and spread the apricot mixture on top. Return to the oven for a further 30 minutes. Mark into bars when well cooked and cool before lifting out.
Bake in oven set at 400 deg F (Mark 6) for 55 minutes altogether.

FAIRY SPONGE CAKES

Ingredients:

3 eggs   3 oz soft brown sugar
3 oz flour   few drops vanilla essence

Method:

Whisk together the eggs and sugar until thick. Fold in the flour and essence and mix well. Place into bun cases. Bake in oven 450 deg F (Mark 8) for 5-10 minutes.

FLAPJACKS

Ingredients:

8 oz margarine   12 oz rolled oats
8 oz demerara sugar   2 tablespoons black treacle

Method:

Beat the margarine and sugar until the mixture is creamy. Stir in the treacle and mix well, add the rolled oats and put in a greased tin. When firm and cooked, cut into fingers and lift out when quite cold.
Bake in oven set at 375 deg F (Mark 5) for 30-40 minutes.

HONEY FLAPJACKS

Ingredients:

4 oz margarine   1 tablespoon honey
3 oz brown sugar   6 oz rolled oats

Method:

Cream together the margarine and sugar and beat in the warmed honey. Work in the rolled oats and spread the mixture in a well-greased shallow tin. Cool before cutting into fingers and leave in tin until quite cold.
Bake in oven set at 350 deg F (Mark 4) for about 40 minutes.

CHOCOLATE COOKIES

Ingredients:

6 oz margarine	12 oz wholemeal s/r flour
6 oz brown sugar	2 oz melted chocolate
1 egg	1½ oz cocoa
milk to mix	

Method:

Mix the margarine and sugar, add the beaten egg, and add the flour and cocoa together. Mix in the melted chocolate and milk to form a stiff dough. Mould into an oblong, wrap in foil or plastic and chill overnight. Slice thinly and put on a greased baking tray when ready.
Bake in oven set at 325 deg F (Mark 4) for 5-10 minutes.

DATE COOKIES

Ingredients:

5 oz margarine	5 oz chopped dates
4 oz brown sugar	8 oz wholemeal s/r flour
1 egg	1 teaspoon vanilla essence

Method:

Mix the margarine and sugar and add the beaten egg and flour. Add the essence and, finally, add the chopped dates and mix well together. Form into an oblong, wrap in foil or plastic and chill overnight in a 'fridge. When needed for use, slice thinly and put on a lightly greased baking tray.
Bake in oven set at 325 deg F (Mark 4) for 5-7 minutes.

MOLASSES COOKIES

Ingredients:

8 oz wholemeal s/r flour	½ teaspoon ground cloves
4 oz margarine	4 oz brown sugar
1 teaspoon ground ginger	1 egg
2 oz molasses	little demerara sugar

Method:

Mix all the dry ingredients together, rub in the margarine, add the sugar and mix in the egg and molasses. Roll into balls the size of walnuts. Dip one side of each into the demerara sugar and place on baking sheet. Bake in oven set at 375 deg F (Mark 5) for 10-12 minutes.

WALNUT COOKIES

Ingredients:

5 oz wholemeal s/r flour	4 oz brown sugar
1 egg	1 teaspoon vanilla essence
2 oz margarine	3 oz chopped walnuts

Method:

Mix the margarine and sugar and add the beaten egg. Add the flour and mix, add the essence and mix-in the chopped walnuts. Form into an oblong, wrap in foil and chill overnight in the 'fridge. Slice thinly and place on greased baking tray when ready. Bake in oven set at 325 deg F (Mark 4) for 10-15 minutes.

ALMOND TARTS

Ingredients:
4 oz shortcrust pastry
4 oz wholemeal s/r flour   water to mix
Filling   2 oz margarine
2 egg whites   2 oz ground almonds
2 oz brown sugar $\frac{1}{4}$ oz ground rice
almond essence   raspberry jam

Method:
Whisk the egg whites until stiff. Mix the ground almonds, ground rice, sugar and a few drops of almond essence together. Fold in the egg whites. Line tart tins with thinly rolled pastry and put a teaspoon of raspberry jam into each centre. Fill with the almond mixture. Bake in oven set at 400 deg F (Mark 6) for 15-20 minutes.

BAKEWELL TART

Ingredients:
4 oz shortcrust pasty
4 oz wholemeal s/r flour   water to mix
Filling   2 oz margarine
1 egg   2 oz margarine
2 oz brown sugar $2\frac{1}{2}$ oz ground almonds
$\frac{1}{4}$ teaspoon almond essence   jam

Method:
Make up the pastry and roll out and line a sandwich tin. Spread the base with raspberry jam. Cream the margarine and sugar and add the beaten egg. Beat in the essence and fold in the ground almonds. Put on top of the jam. Roll out the pastry scraps, cut into thin strips and place on top, lattice fashion.
Bake in oven set at 350 deg F (Mark 4) for 30 minutes.

ALMOND SPONGE

Ingredients:

Sponge

4 eggs	6 oz brown sugar
4 oz margarine	3 oz wholemeal s/r flour
4 oz ground almonds	almond essence

Filling

4 oz margarine	4 oz brown sugar
2 oz ground almonds	few drops almond essence

Method:

Mix the margarine and sugar and add the flour and ground almonds together. Add the egg yolks and a few drops of essence. Whisk the egg whites until stiff and gently fold into the mixture. Place in sponge tin. Cook and cool. Mix the filling ingredients well together and spread in the middle of sponge.

Bake in oven set at 400 deg F (Mark 6) for 30-35 minutes.

CHOCOLATE SPONGE

Ingredients:

4 oz margarine	milk to mix
2 eggs	4 oz brown sugar
4 oz wholemeal s/r flour	3 drops vanilla essence
	1 oz cocoa

Method:

Cream the margarine with the sugar and add the essence. Beat in the eggs one at a time, beating well, fold in the flour and cocoa and lastly the milk till a dropping consistency is obtained. Put in a greased sandwich tin.

Bake in oven set at 400 deg F (Mark 6) for 35-40 minutes.

EASTER BISCUITS

Ingredients:

3 oz margarine	1½ oz raisins or currants
3 oz brown sugar	1 teaspoon mixed spice
1 egg yolk	6 oz wholemeal s/r flour

Method:

Cream the margarine and sugar and beat in the egg and fruit. Mix and add the flour and spice. Mix to a stiff dough using a little milk if it is needed. Roll out on a floured board, prick all over, cut out with a biscuit cutter and place on a greased baking sheet.
Bake in oven set at 350 deg F (Mark 4) for 15-20 minutes.

HONEY GINGER NUTS

Ingredients:

6 oz wholemeal s/r flour	1 dessertspoon ground ginger
2 oz margarine	1-2 tablespoons honey

Method:

Mix the flour and ground ginger and rub in the margarine and honey to make a pliable dough. Roll into rounds, place well apart on a greased baking tin and flatten slightly.
Bake in oven set at 350 deg F (Mark 4) for 15-20 minutes.

EASY WHOLEMEAL BREAD

Ingredients:

1½ lb plain wholemeal flour   2 teaspoons salt
3 teaspoons brown sugar   6 teaspoons dried yeast or
¾ pint warm water   1 oz fresh yeast

Method:

Put the flour, salt and 2 teaspoons sugar in a warm basin. Put the yeast, 1 teaspoon sugar and 1 cup of warm water in a warm place till fermented. Put the fermented yeast in the flour and remaining water and form into a dough. Place in two greased warm loaf-tins and leave in a warm place to double their size, covering with a clean tea towel. When doubled, bake.
Bake in oven set at 425 deg F (Mark 7) for about 30 minutes.

WHOLEMEAL ROLLS

Ingredients:

1 oz fresh or ½ oz dried yeast   ½ pint warm water
1 teaspoon brown sugar   1 lb plain wholemeal flour
1 teaspoon salt

Method:

Put the yeast, sugar and ¼ pint of the water into a large bowl and leave until dissolved and slightly frothy. Mix in half the flour, the salt and the rest of the water, stir well and put the rest of the flour on top, not mixing. Leave in a warm place for 45 to 60 minutes until the mixture has risen and doubled in bulk. Mix in the loose flour and knead for five minutes. Shape into rolls, half the size required for the finished rolls, and place well apart on a greased baking sheet. Cover with a wet cloth and leave in a warm place for 20 to 30 minutes until they have risen.

Bake in a hot oven, 450 deg F (Mark 8), for about 10 minutes, until golden. Place on a wire rack and cool.

MALT LOAF

Ingredients:

1¼ lb wholemeal plain flour	½ teaspoon salt
1 oz fresh yeast or 1 level	2 tablespoons brown sugar
tablespoon dried yeast	1 tablespoon black treacle
¾ pint warm water	1 oz raisins
2 tablespoons milk	

Method:

Mix the flour and salt in a warm bowl, cream the fresh yeast with 1 teaspoon sugar, mix in quarter of a pint water and stir well. Make a well in the flour, add the yeast liquid and stir to make a soft dough. If using dried yeast, sprinkle on quarter of a pint tepid water and leave for 15 minutes until thick and frothy. Stir into flour and knead. Dissolve one level tablespoon sugar with the black treacle and melt in the remaining warm water in a pan, cool and stir in the raisins. Stir into the dough and knead well. Turn the mixture on to a floured board and knead, put back in the bowl, cover with clean warm tea towel and leave in a warm place to rise and double. Knead again on a board. Halve the dough and place portions in two one-pound loaf tins previously warmed and greased. Leave in warm place for 15 minutes to rise. Mix remaining sugar and milk and brush the tops of the loaves.

Bake in oven 450 deg F (Mark 8) for 5 minutes, reduce to 350 deg F (Mark 4) for further 35 minutes.

WHOLEMEAL PLAIT

Ingredients:

1½ lb wholemeal plain flour
2 oz margarine
1 level dessertspoon soft
   brown sugar
¼ pint warm water

½ level teaspoon salt
1 oz fresh yeast or 1 level
   tablespoon dried yeast
¼ pint warm milk

Method:

Sift the flour and salt into a warm bowl, rub in 1 oz margarine. Cream the fresh yeast with the sugar in a basin and stir in the tepid milk and water. Make a well in the centre of the flour and mix to a soft dough with the yeast liquid. If using dried yeast, sprinkle it with the sugar on the tepid liquids and leave for 15 minutes or until thick and frothy. Mix into the flour and knead in bowl until the mixture comes away from the sides. Cover the bowl with a clean, warm damp tea towel and leave in a warm place to rise and double. Grease a baking sheet and turn dough on to a floured board and knead. Form into a plait by dividing the dough into three long shapes of the same size, plait these, sealing each end. Place on the prepared baking sheet and leave in a warm place to swell. Brush the loaf with remaining 1 oz margarine (melted) and bake.

Bake in oven set at 450 deg F (Mark 8) for 10 minutes, then 400 deg F (Mark 6) for further 30-40 minutes.

FRUIT AND LEMON LOAF

Ingredients:

12 oz wholemeal s/r flour	1 teaspoon mixed spice
6 oz margarine	¼ teaspoon salt
4 oz raisins	6 oz brown sugar
grated rind 2 lemons	4 oz cherries
2-3 tablespoons milk to mix	1 tablespoon lemon juice
	3 eggs

Method:

Mix the flour, salt and spice and rub in the margarine until resembling breadcrumbs. Add the sugar, raisins and grated lemon rinds with the eggs. Mix to a soft consistency with the lemon juice and milk, add the halved and floured cherries. Turn into a greased and lined two pound loaf tin.

Bake in oven set at 375 deg F (Mark 4) for 1-1½ hours.

ORANGE LOAF

Ingredients:

10 oz wholemeal s/r flour	6 oz margarine
½ teaspoon nutmeg	1 teaspoon vanilla essence
8 oz brown sugar	4 oz grated chocolate
5 eggs	2 oz chopped nuts
2-3 dessertspoons orange juice	2 grated orange rinds

Method:

Cream the margarine and sugar and add the beaten eggs. Mix in the flour and add the nutmeg, essence, orange rinds, chopped nuts, coarsely grated chocolate and orange juice as required to make a dropping consistency. Put in a greased and lined loaf tin.

Bake in oven set at 400 deg F (Mark 6) for 50-60 minutes.

SCONE MALT LOAVES

Ingredients:

1½ lb brown scone mix	½ pint water
½ teaspoon salt	2 oz margarine
	¼ pint milk

Method:

Grease two round six to seven inch tins. Place the flour in a basin and add the salt, rub in the margarine and when ready add all the liquid mixture. Turn on to a lightly floured board and divide into two equal portions. Mould into rounds and place in tins; flatten tops slightly.

Bake in oven set at 425 deg F (Mark 7) for 25-35 minutes.

SAVOURY SCONES

Ingredients:

6 oz wholemeal s/r flour	¼ teaspoon salt
2 oz margarine	3 oz grated cheese
2 oz rolled oats	1 egg
about ¼ pint buttermilk	1 beaten egg

Method:

Mix the salt and flour and add the margarine, rolled oats and grated cheese. Mix well and add the egg and buttermilk to form a dough. Roll out on a floured board into good half-inch thickness, cut into circles and put on a greased baking tray. Brush with the beaten egg.

Bake in oven set at 425 deg F (Mark 8) for 10-20 minutes.

SCONES

Ingredients:

8 oz wholemeal s/r flour	5 oz margarine
1 oz brown sugar	4 oz raisins
about ¼ pint buttermilk	1 egg
½ teaspoon mixed spice	1 beaten egg

Method:

Mix together the flour and spice and sugar. Add the margarine and mix well. Add the liquid (as reuired), egg and fruit, turn on to a floured board, roll into a good half-inch thickness and cut into rounds. Put on a greased baking tray and brush with the beaten egg. Bake in oven set at 450 deg F (Mark 8) for 10-20 minutes.

DATE SLICES

Ingredients:

½ lb stoned dates	4 oz margarine
1 teaspoon vanilla essence	¼ pint water
6 oz brown sugar	4 oz wholemeal s/r flour
	4 oz oats

Method:

Chop the dates and boil in water till tender. Add the vanilla essence. Mix the oats, flour, sugar and margarine. Put half the mixture into a greased baking tray, spread over with the dates and press on the remaining mixture. When cooked, mark into slices, separating only when cold. Bake in oven set at 400 deg F (Mark 6) for 20-30 minutes.

SHORTBREAD

Ingredients:

6 oz wholemeal s/r flour   2 oz brown sugar
4 oz margarine

Method:

Mix the ingredients together and press into a baking tin, marking into fingers and pricking with a fork.

VARIATIONS added to the above basic mixture.

Ginger Shortbread	1 teaspoon ground ginger
	2 oz chopped crystallized ginger
Cherry Shortbread	4 oz chopped cherries
	½ grated lemon rind
Raisin Shortbread	2 oz chopped raisins
	½ grated orange rind
Nut Shortbread	4 oz chopped almonds
	½ teaspoon ground cinnamon

Bake in oven set at 400 deg F (Mark 6) for 20-30 minutes.

VICTORIA SANDWICH

Ingredients:

6 oz wholemeal s/r flour   3 eggs
6 oz brown sugar   1 dessertspoon top of milk
6 oz margarine   few drops vanilla essence

Method:

Mix the dry ingredients together and add the margarine and eggs with milk and essence until a dropping consistency is reached. Place in two six inch sandwich tins. Bake in oven set at 375 deg F (Mark 5) for 35-40 minutes.

SPICY GINGERBREAD

Ingredients:

¾ lb wholemeal s/r flour
1 teaspoon ground cloves
¼ teaspoon salt
4 oz brown sugar
¾ lb treacle

2 teaspoons cinnamon
3 teaspoons ground ginger
3 oz margarine
1 egg
just under ½ pint hot water

Method:

Cream the margarine and sugar, and add the beaten eggs. Mix well. Add the flour, cinnamon, salt, ground cloves and ginger and mix well. Stir in the treacle and hot water gradually. When smooth pour into a well greased and lined cake tin.
Bake at 400 deg F (Mark 6) for 50-60 minutes.

MADELEINES

Ingredients:

4 oz margarine
4 oz brown sugar
desiccated coconut

4 oz wholemeal s/r flour
2 eggs
raspberry jam

Method:

Beat the margarine and sugar, gradually adding the eggs and a little of the flour. Mix well and stir in the remaining flour. Grease 12 dariole moulds and three-parts fill with the mixture. Bake. When cooked turn out and trim the bottoms so they stand firmly, when nearly cold brush with melted jam and roll in coconut.
Bake in oven set at 375 deg F (Mark 5) for 15-20 minutes.

MACAROONS

Ingredients:

2 egg whites	little egg white
8 oz brown sugar	almond essence
1 oz ground rice	4 oz ground almonds
	split almonds

Method:

Whisk the egg whites until stiff. Stir in the ground almonds and rice, add the essence and mix well with the sugar. Cover a greased baking sheet with rice paper and place the mixture in small heaps on it, leaving room to spread. Place a split blanched almond on each and glaze with egg white.
Bake in oven set at 350 deg F (Mark 3) for 20-25 minutes.

MELTING MOMENTS

Ingredients:

4 oz margarine	5 oz wholemeal s/r flour
3 oz brown sugar	1 egg yolk
crushed cornflakes	vanilla essence

Method:

Cream the margarine and sugar and beat in the eggs and a few drops of vanilla essence. Work in the flour and mix till smooth. With wet hands divide mixture into small rounds and roll into cornflakes. Put on a greased baking sheet.
Bake in oven set at 400 deg F (Mark 6) for 15-20 minutes.

COCONUT SQUARES

Ingredients:

6 oz margarine	4 oz desiccated coconut
4 oz brown sugar	1 egg
4 oz wholemeal s/r flour	1 grated lemon rind

Method:

Cream the margarine and sugar, add the flour and coconut with the beaten egg to bind. Add lemon rind. Roll out on floured board and cut into squares, prick and bake in oven on greased baking tray.

Bake in oven set at 350 deg F (Mark 4) for 15-20 minutes.

WALNUT CRUNCH

Ingredients:

5 oz margarine	6 oz rolled oats
2 tablespoons black treacle	2 oz chopped walnuts
5 oz brown sugar	few drops vanilla essence

Method:

Beat the margarine with the sugar and treacle. Mix in the essence, oats and nuts until smooth. Spread in a shallow square baking tin and press well down. When cool mark into squares. Lift out only when cold.

Bake in oven set at 325 deg F (Mark 3) for 40-50 minutes.

GOLDEN VICTORIA

Ingredients:

4 oz margarine	4 oz brown sugar
2 large eggs	4 oz wholemeal s/r flour
¼ teaspoon vanilla essence	

Method:

Cream the margarine and sugar, add the beaten eggs, mix in the flour and essence. Place in a greased eight inch tin.

Bake in oven set at 400 deg F (Mark 6) for 35-40 minutes.

INDEX

126

127